God's Mission
Spiritual Battles
And
Revelation of Anti-666

Jenness Reid

www.worksoftrinity.com

Published by Works Of Trinity, LLC
Teaneck, New Jersey, 07666, U.S.A.
www.worksoftrinity.com

All scripture quotations are taken from The Holy Bible, King James Version (KJV) – *public domain*.

No part of this book may be reproduced or transmitted in any form or by any means; electronic or mechanical – including photocopying, recording, and information storage and retrieval systems; without written permission from the publisher. Send email to: permission@worksoftrinity.com.

God Mission: Spiritual Battles and Revelation of Anti-666

Copyright © 2014 Jenness Reid, all rights reserved.
Commissioned by Jesus Christ

ISBN-13: 978-0-9831999-2-2 (paperback)
ISBN-13: 978-0-9831999-3-9 (electronic)
Library of Congress Control Number: 2014916534

Dedication

I dedicate this book to the works of The Trinity, which is accomplished by God's children doing His works on earth through the power of God, Jesus, and the Holy Ghost [Spirit]. The goal is to defeat Satan's kingdom on earth and free God's children from his interferences in their lives.

Disclaimer

Everything in this book is based on my life's experiences. The names of actual individuals and places have been changed for identity reasons.

This book is for educational purposes only, and only you are responsible if you choose to do anything, based on what you read.

Jenness Reid

Contents

Preface 6
My Sister, Catreen 8
Spiritual Experiences in the Bible 15
Preparation for God's Mission 32
The Reality of God's Mission 37
The Card Reader 53
Spiritual Incidents on the Bus 59
Spiritual Incidents on the Train 66
Spiritual Incidents at Work 74
Spiritual Incidents at Home 80
Day of the Lamb of God 95
Hospital Experience 104
Post-Hospital Experiences 113
An Extraordinary Life 118
Revelation of Anti-666 147
It Is Not Over 173
Research in Spiritual Psychosis 188
A Message to Church Leaders 204
Bibliography 208

Acknowledgement

I would like to acknowledge the help of God (Adonai), Jesus Christ (Yeshua HaMashiach), and the Holy Spirit (Ruach HaKodesh) for providing guidance in overcoming the many spiritual battles I have been through. They have made Divine contributions to this book by providing its content, through my experiences with Their works.

I give special acknowledgement to my editor, Patsy Quashie. May the favor of God be on her life.

Preface

It might seem strange for someone to speak of being attacked by evil spirits. You will most likely be labeled as being crazy, if you dare to share your experiences. However, if you only take the time to search the Bible, you will find many stories of Jesus casting out evil spirits from people who were sickened in one way or the other by them. Even Jesus' disciples were able to cast out evil spirits in Jesus' name after He gave them the power to do so.

It was a sad day for earth when Satan and his angels were cast out of Heaven. Adam and Eve were the first to fall into Satan's trap. The Bible tells of people working curious arts (satanic crafts), which were documented in books (Acts 19:19), so it continues in our days. People skilled in satanic crafts are inflicting injuries on others, through spiritual means. I am a victim of such spiritual wickedness. This book is about God taking me through His mission of battling evil spirits and conquering them.

Preface

Spiritual wickedness was discovered to be contributing to what was thought to be an all-natural illness, resulting from a car accident. I have been through experiences of outright spiritual battles with the Trinity (God, Jesus, and the Holy Spirit) providing help throughout my ordeals. I was exposed to different levels of evil spirits and demons and had the revelation of how to handle the Biblical *"mark of the beast"* – 666.

Chapter 1

My Sister, Catreen

I cannot write this book without first mentioning what my older sister, Catreen, went through before me. Jesus wanted me to write about her so that her situation can be compared to mine. Catreen is now deceased, but during her late twenties she had been diagnosed as being schizophrenic. To understand what had happened to her, I did an interview with our older sister, Petra, who was around her most of her life.

Catreen's First Experience of Possible Spiritual Attack

While in her teens, one early morning Catreen and Petra were walking to school when Catreen felt a crippling pain from her neck down to her shoulder. Someone took her home while Petra continued to school. When Petra returned home from school there were a lot of church members at the house praying for Catreen.

According to Petra, Catreen perhaps developed this kind of problem due to the physical labor involved in helping our mother to farm the land. Our father died while we were very young and our mother had turned to farming to support us. At the time of Catreen's incident, our mother suspected that she was spiritually attacked, due to the suddenness of the illness and knowing that her enemies would hurt her children to get to her. Catreen was bedridden for a few months. After this, she was not the same. She was afraid of being alone, in case she would experience the same crippling condition. Petra remembered her, before the illness, as a very competitive person. She wanted to be the best in dancing, in school work, in completing housework, and in doing farming.

By talking to my niece, Rose, I was able to get another side of the story surrounding Catreen's sudden illness. Rose mentioned that my mother was a dreamer, like me. I did not know that my mother was a spiritual dreamer until Rose shared with me what my mother told her about her spiritual dream experiences. My mother related to Rose that since her enemies could not overcome her by spiritual means, they went after her children. It was not surprising then that Catreen was the target of attack since she was the most helpful to my mother, at the time.

Rose related to me that my mother told her after Catreen took sick, she prayed to God and saw in a dream that she was to curl over Catreen at nights, as a foul would cover her chicken, to save her life. At nights, during spiritual attacks, my mother would lay curled over Catreen when she sensed that the attacks were coming. When I was young I would see my mother lying curled over Catreen when she was sick, and I thought this was to comfort her.

In my spiritual attack experiences, I realize that most of these attacks occur at nights. With this reality, I presented both the theory of Petra's assessment of Catreen's first major illness and the account of her illness as being spiritually induced, according to my mother's revelation.

Catreen migrated to the United State in her twenties. She had some lingering fears from her past experience but got over it. Catreen got a job at a daycare center where she felt comfortable and gained confidence. She would take the train and bus everywhere by herself, without fear.

Catreen's Second Experience of Likely Spiritual Attack

While living in Jamaica, Catreen used to correspond with a few pen pals from other countries. She got them from magazines. She corresponded with one of them, Elroy from Montserrat, for many years. This continued while she was in the United States of America (U.S.A.). After a while, Elroy asked her to visit him and proposed to marry her. The family discouraged her from going, but she was determined. She went in 1982 and stayed for two weeks.

When in Montserrat, things went well until it was time for Catreen to return. She thought that Elroy drugged her by placing something in her food. She got an engagement ring and she could not remember much else of what happened. She knew that something was done to her. When Catreen came back to the U.S.A., she was never the same. She was fearful of people. She did not trust anyone and thought that she was being stalked by Elroy.

Our sister, Evelyn, decided to take Catreen to the doctor. She was diagnosed with schizophrenia. This diagnosis caused her to feel worse about herself. She thought that the doctors were against her and that Elroy had something to do with her situation. She visited a card reader who indicated that Elroy was doing something to her, through spiritual means. The family did not listen to her when she tried to tell them this. My sisters who she was living with at the time remembered that she had what they thought was a nerve problem, while in Jamaica, and attributed all the problems she was experiencing to this. Furthermore, they had the attitude of rejecting anything suggesting that the cause was from spiritual mean. That was something considered to be "old-time belief" and should be avoided.

Catreen's condition deteriorated to the point where she had to be hospitalized. While there, she was sent to programs to help her. She did not like the idea of taking medicines for the rest of her life. While on medication she got better for a while. However, she was concerned with the side effects and the additional medications needed to counteract them. She was constantly in and out of mental hospitals. Maybe if the drugs did not have such side effects she would have been more accepting of them.

Catreen lost hope in life. Thinking of her financial situation, her missed opportunities because of illness brought about by spiritual wickedness, and her unfulfilled desire to succeed, sometimes made her regress in the illness. Her hope of a better life in the U.S.A. was shattered. At times, no one would be able to tell that

Catreen had a mental illness. However, the family knew when Catreen's sickness was returning. Additionally, stressful situation, such as the death of our mother triggered the illness.

Catreen's Inspiring Dreams

A few months before dying, Catreen had two powerful dreams about our mother and me. In the first dream, our mother told her that my back problem was caused by heavy lifting, not by the car accident. She said that I would get better. In a follow-up dream, our mother showed Catreen what fruits I should use to make tea and drink as the cure for my back problems.

Both Catreen and I were ecstatic about her dreams which were related to my back problem. With a lot of determination, I was constantly trying many different things to get rid of my back problem. However, it was a roller coaster ride. I got some relief here and there. I did not hesitate to pursue getting the tea that Catreen dreamt about. Before she died, she was able to hear about the benefit I had from drinking the tea.

Catreen's After-life Role

After dying, Catreen became a very powerful angel who, along with our mother helped to fight evils spirits that came to attack me. Before I experienced outright spiritual attacks, Catreen prepared my sister, Ruth, and I through dreams that something "big" was going to happen to me (Reid 102). Catreen even went to the point of allowing me to feel the sensation of "being in a crazy state," in a dream, so that I would recognize the threshold of my mental state (Reid 119). She, as well as our mother, made sure that through many dreams to me and other family members, we would recognize situations when I was under spiritual attack and not attribute it to mental illness.

After all, the outcome with Catreen could have been different if the family had recognized that some of the problems she was having was due to spiritual attacks. She would not have gone into an outright mental state. I knew that because of this, she was determined that I would not fall into the same trap as she did. After God warned us of the deaths of our relatives and then let us know that they made it to be with Him after they died; He then used them to help prepare my sisters and I to go through spiritual battles as part of His mission, as indicated in a dream (Reid 68).

Chapter 2

Spiritual Experiences in the Bible

God first used dreams to show me, warn me of, and reveal to me, future events, which included spiritual attacks. These reality dreams (Reid) were followed by outright spiritual attacks. In these spiritual attacks, God was there every step of the way to defend me and direct my defense. These amazing experiences led me to search the Bible to see how Jesus and others dealt with evil spirits in His days. This will set the stage for what I am about to reveal of my real-life experiences.

The Coming of Evil to Earth

I found that evil existed in Heaven and was cast down to earth, therefore putting us in jeopardy. It was revealed to John that war broke out in Heaven. Michael and his angels fought against the dragon and his angels, but the dragon was defeated. The dragon, called a serpent, the Devil, or

Satan was cast out from Heaven with his angels. It is a terrible thing for the earth because Satan is very angry and will deceive many. He knows that he has a short time on earth. However, he can be overcome by the blood of the Lamb (Jesus Christ) and the word of your testimony (Revelation 12:7-12). Jesus told His followers that He saw when Satan fell like a lightening from Heaven (Luke 10:18).

John saw in a vision how the fall of Satan from Heaven will affect earth. He *"saw an angel come down from Heaven, having the key of the bottomless pit"* and a heavy chain in his hand. He caught hold of the dragon, called the Devil or Satan, and chained him up for a thousand years. He was thrown into the bottomless pit, locked and sealed so that he would not deceive the nation anymore until the thousand years are up. After the thousand years he will be loosed for a while. He would go out and deceive the nations all over the world. He would bring them together to do battle; as many as the sand of the sea. The devil, who deceived them would be thrown into Hell where the beast and false prophets would also be thrown (Revelation 20:1-10).

Evil can come to us in the form of punishment. God uses evil spirits to punish people. For example, God sent evil spirit between Abimelech and the men of Shechem so that there was treachery among them (Judges 9:23); Saul was troubled by an evil spirit from the Lord after the spirit of the Lord departed from him (1 Samuel 16:14). This evil spirit was removed after David played his harp while the evil spirit was upon Saul (1 Samuel 16:23).

Even righteous men of God sometimes yield to evil influence. David was provoked by Satan to count the number of people in Israel, which he did. God became displeased with David and punished him by causing an outbreak of disease on Israel, which killed seventy thousand men (1Chronicles 21:1-14).

Being Tested by God

God sometimes allows Satan to have power over us to test our loyalty to Him. Satan showed up before God and told Him that he had been roaming the earth. God asked Satan if he had noticed His servant, Job, who was perfect, righteous, feared Him, and avoided evil. Satan told God that Job was like that because he benefited from God's protection of him, his family, and everything he owned. Furthermore, God had blessed all that Job had so that they increased. Satan suggested that Job would curse God if He took away what Job had. God gave Satan power over what

Job had and told him not to touch Job himself. Satan caused Job's children, animals, and servants to die, except for a few servants who brought the news to Job. In all of this, Job did not curse or blame God, but accepted the situation and worshiped God (Job 1:6-22).

Another day, Satan showed up before God after roaming the earth. Again, God asked Satan if he had noticed his servant, Job, who was perfect, righteous, feared Him, and avoided evil even though Satan had attacked him after God gave Satan permission. Satan told God that a man would give up everything to save his life and if God should hurt his body, Job would curse Him. In response, God allowed Satan to have power over Job, except that he should not take his life. Satan inflicted sores on Job, from his head to his feet. However, Job refused to curse God, even when his wife told him to do so (Job 2:1-10).

Dealing with Evil

People of God can destroy the dwelling places of Satan. Josiah became king of Judah at the young age of eight. Unlike his evil grandfather and father who were kings before him, at age sixteen Josiah followed the example of his ancestor, King David, and worshipped God in a way that was pleasing to Him.

At age twenty, Josiah destroyed the pagan places, symbols of other gods and idols. He gave orders to destroy the altar where Baal was worshiped and tear down surrounding incense altars. By Josiah's orders, the dust of the images of gods and idols were scattered on the graves of those who had sacrificed to them. Josiah *"burned the bones of the pagan priests on the altars where they had worshiped."* By his actions, he made Judah and Jerusalem ritually clean. He did the same cleansing in other cities and throughout the Northern Kingdom. Josiah gave orders to repair the Temple of the Lord God (2 Chronicles 34:1-7).

The Evil State of Earth

What was revealed to John about the state of the earth and the evil that dwell within? A third of humans was killed by three plagues. Those who were not killed did not repent of what they had made and continued to worship devils, and idols of gold, silver, brass, stone, and wood which cannot see, hear, or walk. They did not repent of their murders, magic, sexual immorality, or thefts (Revelation 9:18-21). John saw three unclean spirits that looked like frogs come out of the mouth of the dragon, and out of the mouth of the beast, and out of the mouth of the false prophet. They were the spirits of devils that performed miracles. These three spirits go out to bring the kings of the world together for the battle of the great day of God Almighty (Revelation 16:13-14).

John saw another angel come down from Heaven with great power and the earth was brightened with his glory. The angel cried with a loud voice, saying, *"Babylon is fallen, and is become the habitation of devils and evil spirit. All kinds of filthy and hateful birds live in her"* (Revelation 18:1-2).

When will all this rampage of evil spirits, devil worship, and abandonment of God end? The Lord told Zechariah that there would come a time when He would cleanse the descendants of David and the people of Jerusalem from their sins and uncleanness. The names of idols and the desire to worship them would be gone; false prophets and unclean spirits would be taken from the land. If anyone insisted on prophesying, their own mother and father would tell them that they should not live since they were telling lies in the name of the Lord. In those days people would be ashamed to identify themselves as prophets and would not try to deceive people (Zechariah 13:1-5).

The Works of Jesus – Dealing with Evil Spirits

Jesus was made lower than angels so that He could die for us and that through death He could destroy the devil that had power over death (Hebrew 2:9-14). Jesus came to earth to save us so that one day we would join Him in Heaven. When He came to fulfill His promise of redemption, He had to deal with the evils that were on this earth. He not only healed those who were naturally sick but cast out evil spirits and devils (sometimes called demons these days) out of people who were sick because of being possessed by them.

As when Jesus was on earth, people are still being possessed by evil spirits and devils. We need to pay attention to the many examples of Jesus dealing with evil spirits and devils.

Peter spoke about *"God anointing Jesus of Nazareth with the Holy Ghost [Spirit] and with power,"* allowing Him to go about doing good, and healing all who were oppressed of the devil because God was with Him (Acts 13:34-38).

Jesus cured many people of their sicknesses and plagues. He gave sight to the blind and drove out evil spirits (Luke 7:21). Women have been healed of evil spirits, including Mary Magdalene, from whom seven devils were driven out (Luke 7:2). A woman, who was Greek and Syrophoenician by nationality, had a daughter who had an unclean spirit in her. The woman sought out Jesus and begged Him to cast out the devil from her daughter. When Jesus hesitated, and told her that it was not right to feed the children's food to the dogs, she responded by faith and told Him that the dogs usually ate the leftovers. Because of her faith, Jesus removed the devil from the woman's daughter in the same hour (Mark 7:25-30; Mathew 15:22-28).

While in a crowd of people, a man came and knelt before Jesus, begging Him to heal his son who was an epileptic and often had such bad attacks that he sometimes falls into the fire and the water. It caused his son to get into a fit, foam at the mouth, tear, and bruise himself. The evil spirit would hardly let go of the man's son. The man had brought his son to Jesus' disciples, but they could not heal him. While the son was on his way to Jesus, the devil threw him down into a fit. After Jesus rebuked the devil, the boy was cured immediately. The disciples then asked Jesus why they could not heal the boy. Jesus told them that they did not have enough faith. If they had faith as little as a mustard seed, they could do anything. However, Jesus said that the kind of devil in the boy was one that would not go out unless there was prayer and fasting (Mathew 4:24, 17:14-21; Luke 9:37-42).

Jesus became famous throughout Syria. People brought to him those with all kinds of diseases, mental disorders, epileptics, and those who were possessed by devils. He healed them all (Mathew 4:24).

When Jesus was in the synagogue teaching, a man came in with an unclean spirit. The unclean spirit within the man screamed out, asked Jesus to leave them alone and asked what He wanted with them. The unclean spirit identified Jesus of Nazareth and asked if He came to destroy them. They said that they knew that Jesus was the Holy One of God. Jesus ordered the unclean spirit to be quiet and come out of the man. The unclean spirit shook and bruised the man before coming out of him, with a loud cry.

The people in the synagogue were amazed and wondered what authority Jesus had that even unclean spirits obeyed Him. After Jesus left the synagogue, people continued to bring those who had diseases and those that were possessed with devils to Him. Jesus healed the sick and cast out devils; while doing so He asked the devils not to identify Him because they knew who Jesus was. After a while, Jesus went back into the synagogue and continued to cast out devils (Mark 1:23-39; Luke 4:32-41).

One Sabbath when Jesus was teaching in the synagogues, He saw a woman who had been sick with an evil spirit for eighteen years. The evil spirit kept her bent over and she could not straighten up. Jesus called the woman to Him and told her that she was loosed from her sickness. Jesus placed His hands on her and immediately she was able to straighten up. She gave God the glory. The Pharisees were displeased that Jesus did this work on the Sabbath (Luke 13:10-14). They asked Him to leave because Herod would kill him. Jesus referred to Herod as a fox and told the Pharisees to tell him that He cast out devils and cured the sick today and tomorrow and would finish on the third day (Luke 13:31-32).

Jesus met a man who had devils for a long time, which caused him to go naked and lived in the tombs. Whenever this man was caught and tied up, the unclean spirit would allow him to break loose from the chains and fetters and would drive him into the wilderness. Jesus commanded the unclean evil to come out of the man. The unclean spirit within the man allowed him to fall before Jesus and cried out, *"Jesus, thou Son of God most high."* The unclean spirit begged Jesus not to punish him. Jesus asked the unclean spirit his name. He said that his name was Legion, since there were many devils in the man. The devils asked Jesus not to command them go out into the deep. Instead, they wanted to go into a herd of swine. They left the man and entered the swine, causing them to get violent and run into a lake where they were choked. People came and saw the man who was once possessed with devils, clothed and in his right mind. The man later publicized throughout the town, what Jesus had done for him (Mathew 8:16-33; Luke 8: 27-33; Mark 5:1-20).

Jesus and his disciples were with a large crowd of people from Judaea, Jerusalem, and the coastal cities of Tyre. They came to hear Him and to be healed of their diseases. Many of the people were troubled by unclean spirits and Jesus healed them (Luke 6:17-18). A crowd of people followed Jesus as He had healed many. Some of them had plagues and unclean spirits. When the unclean spirits saw Jesus, the people whom they were in would fall before Him and called out that He was the Son of God (Mark 3:10-11).

Mistaken Works of God

Since people were aware of the power of the devil, they sometimes mistook the works of God for the works of the devil. John the Baptist and Jesus experienced this problem. Many people thought that John the Baptist had a devil because he neither eat bread nor drink wine (Luke 8:12; Mathew 11:18). The works of Jesus also came under much questioning by religious leaders.

A man who had a devil that caused him to be blind and dumb was brought to Jesus. After Jesus healed him, he could see and speak. When the Pharisees heard of this they said the Jesus was casting out devils by the power of Beelzebub, the prince of the devils, while others wanted to see a sign from Heaven.

Jesus explained that if Satan cast out Satan then his kingdom was divided against itself. However, if Jesus cast out devils by the Spirit of God, the kingdom of God had come to the people. Jesus further explained that when an unclean spirit left someone, he would walk through dry places seeking rest. When he did not find any rest, he would decide to go back to the body which he was in. When he finds that the body is clean and purified he will go and get seven other spirits that are worse than him and then come back to live in that body. This makes the individual worse than the state he was in when he first had the one unclean spirit (Mathew 12:22-45; Luke 11:26; Mathew 9:32-34).

Sometimes the work of God is so amazing and so intense that you forget about yourself and others might think that you are mad. This was the case with Jesus when He was too busy to eat while healing people. A large crowd followed Jesus and His disciples. They had no time to eat as they were busy healing and casting out evil spirits. The scribes from Jerusalem said Jesus had Beelzebub in Him and that it was this prince of the devils that gave him the power to cast out devils. Jesus told them that Satan would not drive out Satan because if Satan rose up against himself, his kingdom would fall apart. Jesus' mother and brother came to take charge of Him. They thought He had gone out of his mind because He was not eating, and people were saying that He had an unclean spirit (Mark 3:20-31). When Jesus was teaching in the temple He asked the people why they were seeking to kill Him. The people replied that He had a devil in Him who was trying to kill Him (John 7:14-20).

While Jesus was teaching in the temple, He told the people that if God was their Father they would have loved Him for He came from the Father who sent Him. Jesus told them that their father was the devil who was a murderer and a liar. They did not hear God's word because they were not of God. The Jews then told Jesus that He was a

Samaritan and had a devil. Jesus told them that He did not have a devil but honor the Father and that they were dishonoring Jesus. He told them He did not seek His own glory. If they kept His words they would never die. The Jews then told Jesus that Him saying that convinced them that he had a devil (John 8:47-52).

After Jesus told the Jews that He would lay down His life that He might take it again; He had the power to lay it down and take it again; many of them said that Jesus had a devil and was mad. They questioned why they should listen to Him. Others said His words were not of the devil and questioned if a devil could open the eyes of the blind (John 10:17-21).

I have pointed out cases where, in the days of Jesus, people were wrongfully attributing the power of Jesus Christ to the devil. Since Jesus Christ had taken on the body of human, some people had a hard time understanding that the Spirit of the Almighty God can accomplish great and mind-boggling works, while in human body. People are looking for purely spirit form to accomplish the works of God. Such people will miss the opportunity of getting help from the Almighty God, by His power [Holy Spirit] working through human beings.

The Works of Jesus Continues

The works of Jesus continue through others – from Biblical days to now. He gave His twelve disciples the power to heal sicknesses and cast out devils. He told them to go to those with unclean spirits and to the lost sheep of Israel and preached that the kingdom of Heaven was at hand. The disciples cast out many devils and anointed, with oil, many that were sick, and healed them (Mark 3:14-15; Mark 6:7-13; Luke 9:1; Mathew 10:1-8). John told Jesus that he saw a man casting out devils in Jesus' name and he told him not to do so because he was not one of Jesus' disciples. Jesus told John not to forbid the man because he was not against them (Luke 9:49-50; Mark 9:38-40).

Jesus appointed seventy followers to preach the word of God and to heal the sick. They returned very happy, telling Jesus that even the devils obeyed them when they commanded them in His name. Jesus told them that He saw when Satan fell like a lightening from Heaven. He then gave the seventy followers powers to walk on serpents and scorpions and to overcome the enemy and promised that nothing would hurt them. Jesus cautioned them that they should not rejoice that they had power over spirits, but to rejoice because their names were written in Heaven. Jesus was happy in His Spirit and gave God thanks that He had given to the uneducated what He had not given to the wise and educated (Luke 10:1-21).

After Jesus was raised from the dead He appeared to Mary Magdalene from whom He had cast out seven devils. Jesus then appeared to His eleven disciples and told them that those who believe in Him would cast out devils in His name and speak with new tongues (Mark 16:9-17).

Jesus appeared to Saul and made him a minister and a witness for God. He instructed Saul to go to the Gentiles to turn their darkness to light; deliver them from the power of Satan; and bring them to God, so that their sins can be forgiven, and they can inherit the Kingdom of God, through their faith (Acts 26:14-18).

Many sick people were brought to Peter for healing; some of them had evil spirits in them. They were all healed (Acts 5:15-16).

God allowed Paul to perform miracles to heal people from their diseases; some of them were cured by driving out evil spirits that caused their sicknesses. Seven sons of the Jewish High Priest, Seva, were exorcists. They decided to try to drive out evil spirits from a man, in the name of Jesus, like Paul. The evil spirit told them that he knew Jesus and Paul and asked who they were. The man with the evil spirit then attacked them violently and overpowered them in such a way that all their clothes were torn off and they were left wounded. This caused fear among the people. Many people confessed what they had done and those that practiced magic brought their books together and burned them in public (Acts 19:12-19).

Philip preached about Christ in Samaria. The people paid attention to what he was saying as they listened to him and saw the miracles he performed. Unclean spirits came out of many people, crying out loud as they went. Many who were paralyzed and lame were also healed (Acts 8:5-7).

Stay Humble with Your Gifts

Even though we may be given the gift to heal others and cast out evil spirits and devils (demons), it is wise to stay humble. Paul talked about his visions and revelations given to him by the Lord about a man caught up to Heaven. Of this he would boast, but not about himself. He mentioned that he was given an ailment which acted as Satan's messenger to keep him from being proud because of the abundance of revelations God was giving him (2 Corinthians 12:1-7).

Chapter 3

Preparation for God's Mission

In the previous chapter, I shed some light on the existence of evil spirits and devils [demons] since Biblical days. I can now go into details of my experiences with what I call *"spiritual wickedness."* It was necessary for me to go through these practical experiences to complete God's mission for my life. This is to expose the works of Satan and to help those who are going through similar experiences.

Before I experienced the most serious aspects of God's mission, He prepared me with dreams that caught my attention. Things then progressed to outright fights with evil and demonic forces; and lead to a revelation of how to counteract the Biblical *"mark of the beast"* – 666. I was never alone in the fight. God provided help along the way in one form or another.

In the dream stage, I started having dreams in which many of them were fulfilled. After seeing the fulfillment of a dream about two pregnant co-workers, I started keeping a journal of my dreams. My sister, Ruth, was also having dreams with many being fulfilled. I was able to record a few of her dreams. We were also having an unusual amount of dreams involving our deceased mother. It was as if she was trying to tell us something.

One of Ruth's outstanding dreams is about *Peter Jennings, the then recently deceased newscaster, interviewing our mother. Ruth could tell that something really news worthy had happened in the family* (Reid 109-110). Another dream which also supports the indication of something really big happening in the family, is about *our mother bawling and rolling on the floor in grief as a group of family members gathered around her and watched. Ruth asked her for six months to deal with it* (Reid 99-100). This six months, as calculated, was January 2008.

Yet another more direct dream that foretold of something happening to me is a dream in which *my deceased sister, Catreen, told Ruth that all the dreams were about me* (Reid 101). In another dream, *Catreen told Ruth that something big was going to happen in January* (Reid

102). Again, this pointed to January 2008, which indeed turned out to be the start of intense spiritual attacks on me.

Catreen's Death Influence on Dreams Dynamics

The dynamics of the dreams Ruth and I were having changed drastically after our sister, Catreen, died. It was as if she was frantically trying to warn us about something. In a dream, *she told that they were very worried on the other side* (Reid 108). Many my dreams were about *me being aware of evil spirits coming around, or after me.*

At some point, Ruth and I started to have some dreams in parallel about the presence of evil. On two significant nights, we both dreamt closely related dreams. We both dreamt on the same night about *tombs* and on another same night we dreamt about *a frog and death*. I even saw my *"Heavenly number"* in the frog dream (Reid 116).

It was becoming clear to Ruth and me that we were being warned that one of us was going to die. We accepted this and decided to take out additional life insurance so that at least our family would benefit. After Ruth dreamt Catreen in which she told her that all the dreams were about me, I spoke to both of my daughters and told them to be prepared for my death. I spoke to them about being independent and to be able to take care of themselves. My soul was in good shape, but I made sure that I stayed focused on God.

Spiritual Battle

Before I entered spiritual battle, God had somewhat prepared me as well as my close relatives, with reality dreams that were fulfilled in real, or, relative ways. God wanted us to pay attention to our dreams. It was through dreams that He indicated to me that I would completely recover from my back problems. The many reality dreams are written about in the book, *God Works Through Dreams* (Reid). This book contains dreams about the upcoming deaths of my mother and sister; Mariah Carey singing with me; dining with Jewish family; Jewish family coming to church; the upcoming God's mission; the deceased newscaster, Peter Jennings; and much more.

When the dreams turned into the ugly reality of outright evil and demonic attacks in January 2008, my sister, Ruth, and I were not too surprised. However, we were not prepared for what we were dealing with. Hence, I sought the help of a card reader to explain what was going on and to help ward off evil spirits. However, I soon found out that I only needed the power of the Almighty God alone to take care of every evil attack and He was always *"on time."* The card reader could not help me in what I was facing. She only served to confirm that I was being attacked by evil spirits.

Chapter 4

The Reality of God's Mission

The reality of God's mission came in the form of spiritual attacks by satanic forces; with God defending me throughout my ordeals. Things took a turn when my daughter, Sonia, told me that she dreamt about her deceased aunt, Catreen. In the dream, *Catreen was lying on Ruth's bed as if dead. She then turned to Sonia with a very angry look and said, "I didn't have to die. They could have saved me"* (Reid 103).

With this new dream and the direct dream that Ruth had earlier of Catreen telling her that all the dreams we were having were about me, Ruth and I both concluded that Catreen was desperately trying to tell us something and that we needed help in finding out what it was.

The Quest to Interpret the Dreams

Ruth and I began to suspect that voodoo, or obeah was involved in what I was experiencing because of the types of dreams we were having. Although we normally despise seeking help with such matters, we decided that Catreen was trying much too hard for us not to take some action. I had already accepted that I was going to die soon. I told my two daughters that it was I who was going to die; before we were not sure if it was Ruth, or me. After Catreen pointedly told Ruth that all the dreams we were having was about me; we knew for sure that I was the one to die. My soul was ready. Daily, I would pray and play my Christian music when I was home and while driving.

I told a friend about the kinds of dreams my family and I were having. She agreed that it seemed that voodoo was involved. She searched the internet and found a name that I could use to search for information about voodoo. She said that if it was voodoo, it was only someone who knew about that could take it away; otherwise, it would kill me.

On January 12, 2008, I went to see my sister, Ruth, to discuss what was happening to us with the then more frequent dreams that depicted death threat, or something of a serious nature. While at Ruth's house, I decided to search the internet for the website to check out symptoms of voodooism. As soon as I clicked on one of the links from the search result, I felt a force pushing me away from the computer. It was more like the feeling of the wind pushing against me, but not blowing. I quickly clicked away from the website and closed the browser. Immediately the force stopped. To test out what had just happened, I decided to go to other sites I used to visit, such as Yahoo. There was no such reaction. I decided that I was being prevented from contacting voodoo people. God did not want me to get involved with them.

Later that day I went to a card reader, a Puerto Rican who was Catholic and believed in God. I used to hear Catreen speak of her; that she visited her to clarify what was happening to her, when she was going through spiritual attacks. The rest of us sisters had condemned Catreen for doing this. After selecting cards that the card reader shuffled, she started reading them and told me what she was seeing.

The card reader told me that a woman was using spirits to try to separate my husband and me and that our house was involved. She told me where this woman lived and gave other information which could point to someone I heard my husband spoke of many times, even though I did not meet her.

The card reader told me that because I was spiritual (meaning that my spirit could tell when there was spiritual interference with me) my deceased relatives could communicate with me and try to show me what was happening; I was dreaming but did not understand my dreams. The card reader said that they had a voodoo doll of me with a collar around the neck and a metal sticking through the neck; and that they buried me spiritually in a cemetery besides an old grave. I then told her of the dreams I had. One dream was about *me lying and hugging an old tomb* and another was about *a lady with a collar around her neck and a piece of metal sticking through her neck* (Reid 119-120, 114). She said that swelling in my legs and pelvic area was to prevent me from having sex with my husband. He was supposed to get fed up and leave me.

All along I was thinking that the welts that saw on my leg were the calcium/magnesium vitamin reaction to the tea I call *"God's herb"* which I was taking for my back problems. Catreen had dreamt about it, before she died, as the cure for my back problems. The reference to my leg problem also reminded me of the dream I had about *very large rat dung (feces) with groves in it, which was outside a rat house*. This dream was followed by real rats literally appearing in my house. This was the very first time I saw rats in my house and it never happened again.

The card reader said I came from a spiritual family and she could not understand why we waited so long to seek help. I left the woman feeling better, at least, knowing what I was dealing with; although I had no idea how to handle the situation. She told me to come back the following Saturday to get some stuff for bathing, which should help keep away evil spirits. In the meantime, she gave me a few bottles of liquid that she had with her until she can get others from the Botanical store.

I did not tell my husband that I went to see a card reader. About the Tuesday of that week, January 15, 2008, I was sleeping when I suddenly woke up. I looked to my left toward where my husband was lying and saw a dark shadow over his face. I knew that it was the shadow of evil. I left the room and went into the next room to sleep. Shortly after I fell asleep, I saw a dark shadow in the form of my husband coming over me as in a sexual position. I call out, "*Jesus….*" and woke up. I knew that it was an evil spirit taking the form of my husband.

That day I went to Barnes & Noble on my way home from work and bought four Bibles. I read Psalm 91 before going to bed and place the Bibles around me, at my head, two sides, and at my feet. I was not sure of how to handle my situation.

Blatant Spiritual Attacks

Since I was having more frequent spiritual attacks at nights in which I had to be calling on Jesus, I decided to purchase more Bibles. On the evening of January 18, 2008, I stopped at Barnes & Noble and bought five additional Bibles. That night before going to bed, I decide to open each Bible to Psalm 91 and taped one on my chest and one on either of my legs. I put one Bible above my head, one on either of my sides, and one at my feet. I knew for sure that I was fighting evil spirit and I was using the Lord as my defense.

I woke up repeating the 23rd Psalm. I was repeating it as fast as an auctioneer. My husband who was sleeping in the room woke up. My daughter, Maud, who was two rooms away also woke up and came into the room to find out what was happening. Although I was aware that they were around, watching, and wondering what was going on, I continued to repeat the 23rd Psalm with lighting speed. I could not stop myself. I knew that I was under spiritual attack and I knew that it was not my natural self who was in control. I heard Maud said that she was going to call her prayer group at her church. The attacked continued for about fifteen minutes before I felt that the evil had left.

As soon as I got the break I called my sister, Ruth, and told her that I was under attack and asked her to pray for me. I told her what happened. She said that she would be reading Psalm 35. I told her that I was going to call my friend, Donna, to pray. I called Donna and told her what happened. She told me to repeat, *"No weapon formed against me shall prosper."* I had the phone to my ears, listening to her, when I came under attack again.

Donna continued to be on the phone while the attack was going on. She asked if I had a Bible close by. I told her, *"Yes."* She told me to read Psalm 91. I started reading Psalm 91 repeatedly, rapidly – like an auctioneer. After a while, I got stuck at repeating only verses 10 to 12, *"There shall no evil befall thee, neither shall any plague come nigh thy dwelling. For He shall give his angels charge over thee, to keep thee in all thy ways. They shall bear thee up in their hands, lest thou dash thy foot against a stone"* (Psalm 91:10 - 12).

The phone was to my ears and the Bible in my other hand while I rapidly repeated those verses. Again, I knew that God's angels had taken over my defense, through me. This continued for fifteen to twenty minutes before I felt free from the presence of evil. When the attack was over, Donna instructed me to go around to every room in the house and read Psalm 91.

I asked Maud to turn on the lights everywhere in the house. I then went to every room, kitchen, living room, and basement and read Psalm 91. My husband and Maud walked with me. Maud commented that whatever it was, it was determined to kill me and that it was bold because in front of them it continued the attack. She told me that it was best if I go to my doctor and get some medicine to help me sleep since so much lack of sleep could drive anyone crazy. I told her that I would go to see a doctor. She was a nurse, so I knew that she had a good understanding of the situation. She had told me that two weeks prior to coming to live with us, she dreamt that *she came to the house and saw her daddy and me sitting on the couch. I was crying, and I told her that something was trying to kill me.* I knew God gave her this dream to prepare her for what she had just witnessed.

I Ran for My Life

Later in the morning I called my sister, Ruth, and asked her if I could stay with her for a while. She told me to come, burn my underwear, leave the other clothes behind, and buy new clothes to change into at the store before coming. I asked Maud to give me a ride to Ruth's house. She said, "*Yes*." I told my husband that I was going to spend some time at Ruth because of the situation I was facing at the house. He said, "*OK*" and did not think much of it. After he left the house I got ready then burned almost all my underwear.

Before leaving for Queens, I asked Maud to stop by Marshall's store where I purchased a few clothes. I changed in the bathroom and threw the clothes I had on in the garbage. On the way to the Queens, Maud and I discussed what happened. I told her the little I learned about the possible source of the evil attacks.

The next day I asked my nephew, James, to take me to my house. I saw my husband and his nephew, Clifford, at the house. They were at the computer as my husband was showing him a Real Estate program on the computer. I called to him and told him that I just came to get my clothes. He said, "*OK*" and did not think anything of it since he was intense on what he was showing Clifford.

I got some black garbage bags and quickly grab my clothes and shoes and then asked James to take them to his car. This was done while my husband and Clifford were deep in discussion and not aware of exactly what I was doing. That reminded me of a dream in which *I told my husband that God was ready for me to go on His mission and he didn't hear or see me. He was too intense on chipping away at a piece of zucchini* (Reid 67-68).

I directed James to a nearby Salvation Army and there I put all my clothes and shoes in the receiving bins. Ruth did not want any of my clothes to go to her house since I told her about the dream I had of *a small lizard coming out of the drawer where I kept my clothes and then jumping at me.* I also remembered an incident when I felt lopsided just after putting on my shoes. On two occasions I had to go to the store and purchase new shoes to get some relief. It was as if just putting on those shoes caused the situation to be so pronounced. I had no idea that my clothing and shoes were being used to launch spiritual attacks on me.

Nowhere Is Safe

Ruth allowed me to sleep in her room while she slept in her daughter's room, with her. The first night I spent there was as if evil spirits caught up with me. It soon became a pattern that after midnight I would find myself defending various parts of my body and calling on Jesus or using the words from God to defend the area under attack. My spirit could sense the attack from evil spirits and would react accordingly. I would defend the part of my body with rapid movement of my hand over the area. The movement would be intense for a while then gradually slow down until it ended. While defending myself, I would repeat the words that God put in my spirit, as my defense.

Most of the attacks were aimed at my face. Other areas of attacks were my head; mouth; throat; heart; belly; my right arm, as if I was being injected; and groin area, specifically on the right side. In one of the attacks, I got up off the bed and crunched at one side of the bed as if hiding from something that came into the room. I heard myself speaking out, "*I will divorce Teddy Dakins*," several times.

My Feet Are Not Mine

Few days after I fled to Ruth's house for refuge, my friend, Donna stopped by to pray for me. She was in the living room talking to Ruth and me when she asked us to be quiet. She then told us the Holy Spirit asked her to get a CD she had in her vehicle.

Donna came back and asked Ruth if she had a CD player. Ruth went and got her CD player. Donna then told us that Holy Spirit said she should play two songs from the CD - *Step on the Enemy* and *Obeah Woman Yu Power*

Catch Cold (Lang, n.d.). I was sitting down; Donna and Ruth were standing when the *Step on the Enemy* song started playing. As it played, we all were singing after it and dancing. Very soon, my feet were trampling at a very rapid pace. I knew I was not in control of them. I said to Donna and Ruth, "*I am not the one doing it.*" I knew that the Holy Spirit had taken control of my feet.

Medical Doctor's Help

The same week I fled to Ruth's house for refuge I went to my medical doctor and explained to her that I could not sleep due to nightmares from attacks by evil spirits. I also mentioned I found out that someone was doing this to separate my husband and me. She asked me about my religious belief and if when growing up I had knowledge of such things. I told her that I heard about Obeah but thought that those were things you stayed away from and therefore would not be bothered by it. As the saying goes, "*Belief kills and belief cures.*"

    I grew up in a Presbyterian church but visited many different churches while going to high school. I was not fussy about belonging to a specific church. I went to church because of God and not because of religion. I told my doctor that the person identified as causing the problems was from her country. She said, *"That's OK."* She explained to me that she would write me a prescription for sleeping pills, but if they do not work I might have to get hospitalized to get a different medication. I told her, *"OK."* I got the idea of what she was talking about. I also asked her if she knew of someone who could help me with my divorce because I intend to divorce my husband. I told her that I wanted to go to psychologist who believed in God. She gave me the name of a psychologist.

Power of the Word

Taking the sleeping pills did not help me to sleep, as I expected, because it could not prevent the attacks of evil spirits and I got awaken when I came under attack. I usually read Psalm 91 before I go to sleep and leave the Bible opened to that Psalm on the bed besides me. I realized that it was not the Bible that scare away evil spirits but the words from it, when spoken. I usually relate to Ruth what happened to me in the night. Some of the nights, she would hear me defending myself.

I realized that the things I got from the card reader to bath with and candles to burn were not effective against the evil spirits. It was always the spoken words of God, which came through my spirit that eventually drove them away. I used words such as, *"Jesus,"* repeatedly; *"Holy Spirit,"* repeatedly; *"Power of God,"* repeatedly; *"God,"* repeatedly, and *"Spirit of God in me,"* repeatedly.

I remembered one evening Ruth gave me a very small book by Charles Capps entitled, *God's Creative Power Will Work For You*. She told me to read it. I must have read only pages 8 and 9 because I was in a hurry to try to fall asleep. I needed to get as much sleep as I could before midnight. I remembered that the author was saying that God's word has power and you were to speak it. That night, I was attacked, as usual. This time it was my throat that God, through my spirit, led me to defend. I was repeating, *"Power of the Word"* until the attack subsided. I put away the book and could not find it again.

Psychologist Help

On February 18, 2008, I went to see a psychologist. I explained to her that I would like to get help going through my divorce since I did not know what was involved. She asked me to explain what was happening. I started telling the psychologist about the evil attacks I had at nights. As soon as I started to say, *"I was able to overcome them by calling on the name of Jesus,"* I felt a refreshing, enlightening movement rising from the lower part of my chest to settle on my face. Tears came to my eyes as I spoke. The psychologist said to me, *"Your face lights up when you speak about Jesus."* She asked me to tell her three positive things about myself. I told her that, *"I care about people; I have the love of God; I am kind and loving."* She wrote what I said on one of her cards and gave it to me. She told me to repeat them twice per day.

I left disappointed that the psychologist was not able to help with divorce information. Before going to the medical doctor, my friend had told be to ask her to recommend a psychologist who knows God. My intention to see the psychologist was for her to help with my divorce. However, God intended for her to see Him display Himself, through me.

From Night to Day

It wasn't too long before the nightly attacks became day and night attacks. It was very rough on me physically because I was still going to work and not getting much sleep for so long. Furthermore, I had to be taking two or three trains, depending on my choice, plus two buses to reach work, since I was now travelling from a different State to my job. I had given my husband my van to use because he had car problems and I could take the bus to work while he couldn't.

Chapter 5

The Card Reader

When I was first encountering outright attacks by evil spirits, I did not know how to deal with it. This led me to visit a card reader to seek help. I soon realized that I was overcoming the attack of evil spirits by using the words of God and by whatever means He led me to defend myself, while under attack. Despite this fact, I made a few visits to the card reader because I felt that I found someone who understood better than me what was going on. I found the constant attacks overwhelming, even though I was overcoming by the power of God, extended to me. I was very concerned that I was not able to get the amount of sleep I desperately needed.

On one occasion when I visited the card reader, I asked her why my ears would clog up quickly after I started a conversation with my husband and not when talking to other people. She told me that it was easy for people to use the phone to do damaging spiritual work. She said that it was only because I was spiritual why I was able to tell when there was spiritual interference on the phone. Other people would be inflicted with spiritual sickness through the phone without knowing when it is being inflicted. They would only see the result. Because of the evil affliction through the phone, I avoided talking to my husband and whenever I had to, I would make the conversation as short as possible.

Spiritual Darkness

Whenever I use the bath liquid from the card reader, which was supposed to keep away evil spirits, I would first take a bath then use it to wash over me. She would try different ones whenever I went back to her since the attacks continued. Before using the liquid, I would stir it and repeat, "*Father, Son, and Holy Ghost*" a few times, seeking God's approval since I wasn't sure what using the liquid meant.

On this one occasion, while stirring the liquid, my spirit cried out, "*No, no.*" It took me by surprise and I started to think that maybe Satan did not want me to protect myself against evil spirits. I was confused. I said, "*Get behind me Satan.*" I then started to use the liquid to wash over me. I suddenly saw that my entire body was being engulfed in darkness. I immediately stopped using the liquid and quickly started showing.

Ruth came into the bathroom and saw me showering. She said, *"I thought you were only supposed to be taking baths."* I told her about the darkness engulfing my body after using the liquid from the card reader. I felt deeply troubled that The Holy Spirit of God was warning me that the liquid was not good to use. However, I thought that it was Satan trying to prevent me from using it.

After I showered, I set my regular bath and stirred the water repeating, *"Father, Son, and Holy Ghost."* After a while my spirit cried out, *"Dear God please forgive me of all my sins."* Soon my spirit spoke out, *"I am redeemed. Thank God I am redeemed."* That made me felt so unbelievably good. I later heard myself spoke out, *"I will help others going through the same thing that I am going through. I am going to write You songs."* My mind was shocked to hear my spirit made such promises. Movements of The Holy Spirit and dealing with evil spirit was new to me. I had no idea of what was happening to me.

It Was Still Too Much

I continued to use the card reader because I felt that it was too much for me to handle, not thinking that God was always there handling it with me. I believe that I owe God a sincere apology for continuing to use the card reader even when it was clear that it was Him who was getting rid of the evil spirits. *Heavenly Father, my Lord and God, Adonai, I ask Your forgiveness for visiting the card reader after You pointed out to me that You are the One Who is defending me. I acknowledge You here by Your Hebrew name, Adonai – the name that by which You requested to be called.*

I was continuously bombarded with all different forms of evil spirits. I could see them in the form of dark shadows when it was night or clear heat wave-like shadows in the day. I got attacked by these shadows sometimes when I opened the closet door to take out my coat; sometimes at the entrance of the door when I was leaving or entering the house; and sometimes in the bathroom as I entered in. These shadows would immediately come upon my body and I could feel the ache as they penetrated my body.

Another form of evil spirit was those that attached to my clothing and when I put on my clothes they would penetrate my body. It was as if whoever, was sending evil spirits to attack me was doing it non-stop and by whatever means to kill me.

The Card Reader

One day I felt so bombarded and suffocated with evil spirits that I decided to seek the help of the card reader to see if she could relieve me of them. At this point, I had come to realize that it was God Who was truly allowing me to overcome the evil spirits. However, that day the intensity of the attack was unbearable. I sat in front of the card reader and she told me to cover my eyes while she sprayed something from a can towards my face and spoke to the evil spirits to leave me. While she was doing that, my spirit took over and I started to say, "*In the name of Jesus*," repeatedly. The card reader started to repeat, "*In the name of Jesus*" with me. Soon I started to feel relieved.

I realized that God wanted to show the card reader that He was the One in charge and doing the work of getting rid of the evil spirits that were attacking me. This reminded me of when Jesus chose to reveal to the psychologist, by radiating my face as I spoke of Him, telling the psychologist that He was the one helping me to overcome the evil spirits.

I knew that this card reader believed in God and Jesus. This made me comfortable going to her. However, I did not understand that her spiritual methods were from the Kingdom of Darkness. It is not good to be ignorant of these things, as I was during the early stages of dealing with spiritual attacks. I thank God that He took a stance against me visiting her for the relief of evil spirit attacks.

Chapter 6
Spiritual Incidents on the Bus

God warned me that I would be spiritually attacked on the bus before it started. One night I got a short sleep. I dreamt that, *I was at the bus stop waiting for the bus when two cats appeared and came up to me. I knew that they were evil spirits in the form of cats. I stepped on one and then they both left.*

Show Your True Self

Soon after the bus stop and cats dream, I realized that the cats were symbolic of evil spirits and that this dream was warning of encounters with evil spirits on the bus. One of the buses I usually take had a bus stop across from where I worked. One evening, I went on the bus and sat down. Two women close to fifty years old, a young woman, and a man in his forties came on the bus. They were all Blacks. The young woman was dressed in black and white coat and black and white-water boots. My spirit recognized them as having evil spirits that were against me.

They started to converse among themselves. The first thing one of the older women said was that, *"We going to make sure she shows her true self today."* Soon after the conversation started, I find myself making the sign of the cross with my tongue inside my mouth, while it was closed. At the same time, I was repeating the 23rd Psalm in my mind. The content of their conversation related directly to what was currently happening in my life.

Mainly one of the older women talked while the others responded to, added to the conversation, or just laughed. They talked that she bought one-zone bus pass. I knew I had a one-zone bus pass. One of the women continued, *"She is not going to travel two zones today."* As she said that she turned to the driver and said, *"Right Bob."* The name of the taxi driver who I would take to the bridge is *"Bob."* The same woman continued, *"Her sister is going to get tired of her. She is waking up several times at nights, disturbing her. She doesn't know that I have a lot of friends and I am recruiting more every day. She is getting ride to the bridge and gets there at 7 o'clock."* I knew that I was waking up often at nights due to the frequent attacks; that sometimes my sister, Ruth, got disturbed by them; and that I usually get to the bridge at 7 o'clock in the morning.

The talkative woman said, *"She doesn't even know how to dress. Where does she shop? Marshalls?"* When I had left my house the day of the first outright evil attack I had stopped at Marshalls store in the mall to buy a few clothes and changed in the bathroom before leaving for my sister's house. The woman continued, *"She doesn't even like movies. All she listens to is music."*

At that time, I was carrying around my CD player that I programmed to play just two songs from the *"Step on the Enemy"* album (Lang, n.d.). One song is a powerful combination of Psalm 27 and Psalm 91 which spoke about *God being my light and salvation; Jesus taking up His sword and spear to fight for me; of God's angel taking charge over me; and of me fearing no evil.* The other song is about *Jesus crippling the power of the Obeah* (Voodoo, De Lawrence, Black Magic, etc.) *woman and being my only protector* (Lang, n.d.). I would play these songs when travelling. Also, I would leave the song that I come to refer to as *"my battle song,"* which is *"Step on the Enemy,"* playing repeatedly at Ruth's house. I use both songs as part of my defense against evil attacks.

The conversation of the group of evil-possessed people on the bus changed to talk about a *"sugar daddy."* The trend of the conversation was that he was close to fifty years old and had to be working part time, which would not be enough. The talkative woman asked if he was going to draw on his 401K.

I was very relieved when the bus reached my stop. My spirit was fully controlled, and they failed in driving me crazy, as was their intention.

The Black History Incident

After being attacked on the job by evil spirit sucking away the air immediately around me to induce stifling, I was relieved when it was time to leave. I went to the bus stop across the street from my job, which was near a shopping mall.

While waiting inside the mall I saw an old Black lady. My spirit became alerted to her. After I went on the bus, she came behind me. She was asking the driver many questions about how to get to where she was going, causing significant delays. She eventually decided to take the bus. She got off at a mall where a Barnes & Noble store is located. I was relieved to see her go. I was about to get off, but since she got off I decided to wait until the next bus stop.

To my dismay, a young Black woman came on the bus with a black and white colored book having the title, "*Black Students.*" My spirit was alerted to her. She sat reading the book. I was going straight from work to a Black History performance in Manhattan. I stopped the bus two stops later; instead of the next stop. As soon as I stood up to get off, a small Bible and a lipstick from my tightly closed jacket pocket got pitched to the floor. They did not just drop. It was as if they were kicked out. The woman with the book laughed.

I quickly picked up the Bible and lipstick and got off the bus. My spirit directed me to push out the lipstick, break it in half and then throw it in a garbage bin at the bus stop. I waited at the next bus stop for the transfer bus. It was very cold. It seemed as if the scheduled bus did not run on time. I decided to cross the street to take another bus that could connect me to one that would also take me to New York.

After I got on the new bus, a woman laughed and said, "*I was not going to let that bus come. She was there freezing in the cold.*" It was a short ride to the other bus stop. After I got on a smaller bus, a young Black woman seated in front of me turned to me and said, *"Do you know where the Taft Road stop is?"* My spirit got cross, which was surprising. I asked, *"Why do you ask?"* She replied, *"I want to know when to get off."* I said, *"I will let you know."* When the stop was coming up I said to her, *"Taft Road is next."*

The young woman got up. She had on a nurse's uniform and was fat. As soon as she got off the bus, I felt a very strong spiritual pushing away that was suffocating. This stop was near to my house. I had to pass it on my way to and from work. It happened that for the next few weeks as I neared my house on the bus I could feel that same sensation. It was the strong presence of evil at my house.

I arrived at the Black History program late, feeling soaked with evil spirits, and suffocated. I found my sister, Ruth, and the rest of her guests. I was lucky that her friend had a bottle of water and a Granola bar, which he gave to me. I drank the water and used the bottle to spit the slime caused by the evil spirits.

The show was a brilliant performance with sororities and fraternity performing their dances. It was based on an African theme. In one of the performances the dancers were dressed in black and white boots and were making up funny faces as they danced, which included intense staring. Although I had evil spirits trapped within me and was feeling pressed down and suffocated, I was able to appreciate such an outstanding performance.

Chapter 7
Spiritual Incidents on the Train

Like what God did before I started experiencing spiritual attacks on the bus; He warned me that I would be spiritually attacked on the train, before it started. One night I dreamt that, *I was on the train when I saw a lizard looking around. I knew that it was looking for me. It spotted me and started coming towards me. I was sitting down, so I raised my feet up high and cried out as it got close to me. I woke up at that point.*

This dream was a warning of upcoming evil spirit encounters on the train. After this dream, I started to see evil spirits in a few people on the train; sometimes as I go to and from work.

Nails of a Fowl

While going to work, on one occasion I saw an older White man with each of his pinky fingers painted with red nail polish. His finger nails did not look normal. They reminded me of the nails of a fowl.

My spirit alerted me to not take my eyes off him. I was eating some corn chips and as I kept watch on this man I started to make deliberate grinding actions on the corn chips, as directed by the Holy Spirit within me.

Two Novels Incident

One day on my way from work, after I changed trains I went and sat beside a beautiful, fair-skinned young girl. As I sat beside her she took out a book with *"Two Novels"* in the title. She turned to a page and I glanced over to see what she was reading. I saw something about *"…scarred clothing burnt by the wife."* She underlined those words. I could tell that I was meant to see those words. I knew that I had burnt my underwear at my home before I left. I did this because my sister and I had concluded that evil spirits were interfering with my personal belongings.

I glanced some more and saw something about *"…happened in the shower."* Later, I would recall the words about the shower when I was anointed in the shower by the Holy Spirit of God.

Warning about Fire

After the reason for reading about *"shower"* on the train was revealed to me, I met the same girl again on the train. This time she came and sat beside me. She took out a Cosmopolitan magazine and turned to a page. Again, I glance over to see what she was reading. I saw something about a man knocking on the door and the lady let him in because his voice was familiar. He went in and killed her.

As I continued to glance, I saw that the next story had to do with the woman upstairs, fire, and firefighter. I was not able to read properly but somehow, I found myself saying to her, *"I get the message."* She said to me, *"What?"* She then closed the magazine and started to make a phone call.

I reached my stop and got off the train. I concluded that the young girl on the train was an angel sent by God to warn me of things to come. Days later, there were two separate incidents that reminded me of the second encounter with the young girl on the train; one was with my husband coming to the house and the other was with the tenant upstairs creating a smoke condition for which we had to call firefighters.

Relieved by Brut Cologne

On one occasion after having a tough day at work, on my way home I was feeling soaked and suffocated with evil spirits. After I switched to my second train, I sat in front of a white man in his fifties. He had a male pouch across his shoulders. He reached in the pouch and took out a Brut cologne. He rubbed it on his face and over his head. I could smell the fragrance coming towards me. Immediately, I began to feel some relief from the suffocation of evil spirits. I realized that God sent this man to help me out. I was overwhelmed with tears and held my head down to cry.

After I finished crying to know that God care that much for me, I raised my head up and saw that the man was gone. He had done his work.

I Will Live to Declare the Lord's Work

Valentine's Day, February 14, 2008, was the worst day I had at work. I was happy to get away at the end of the day. I left feeling overbearingly pressed down and suffocated with evil spirits.

On my way home in the subway, I decided that this was the day I was going to die. Tears came to my eyes as I acknowledged that this was my last day to live. I knew that my soul was ready to meet my Savior. I remembered I had the insurance bill in my handbag. I wrote on it that I wanted my two sisters to be the beneficiaries.

Next, I took out my CD player, which I usually play. It was programmed to play just my two favorite songs. However, after the first song, I realized that the programming was cancelled. I tried to reprogram it to the two songs; but either I forgot how to do it, or, something was wrong. I decided to give up and let all the songs play. Ever since I got the CD from my friend and the Holy Spirit had directed her to play those two songs for me, I never bothered to listen to the rest of the CD.

One of the other songs that I heard really caused me to cry. It said, *"I shall not die but live and declare the works of the Lord amen."* I realized that God was telling me that I was not going to die as I was thinking but would live to do works for Him.

I called my friend, Donna, and asked her to come and pray for me because I was badly in need of prayer. After she came to where I lived, we talked about what was happening to me. She advised me to go to my doctor the next day and explain to her that I need to go on disability because of what I was experiencing.

Scarred Face

While on disability, one very snowy day, I was on my way to see my doctor when I decided to buy a bus ticket at the bridge instead of paying with exact change. I walked up to the ticket counter. There was a man leaning on the counter. As I get close, the man turned in my direction. I was shocked to see that half of his face was covered in sores, more like what you see after a severe burn. I quickly stepped back and decided against buying the bus ticket.

On my way home from the doctor, while on the train, a light-skinned black man sat in front of me. The Holy Spirit alerted me to keep my eyes on him. After a while, he started to use his hand to rub over half of his face.

In the morning of that day, I had used a face cream, as I had done many times on my face. That evening as I prepared to take my bath, I washed my face with only water to remove the face cream. To my surprise, my face started to burn. I quickly got some Vaseline (petroleum jelly) and put it on my face. When I looked in the mirror, I saw that part of my face over my right eye was red and half of my eyebrow was completely gone.

I realized that the actions of the man at the ticket counter with the scarred face and the other man on the train rubbing his face were supposed to induce severe scaring of my face. However, I was only bruised with minor reddening of my face and removal of half of my eyebrow. Once again, I was victorious over evil. They did not achieve the effect they wanted.

Later, I called my niece, Alma. She had been helpful to me, constantly inquiring about my situation, and encouraging me to be strong. I told her what just happened to my face. She told me that she was also feeling it in her spirit and that her face was also burning her. Throughout all my spiritual ordeals, God provided help for me, whether it is from people on this earth, my deceased relatives, His angels in Heaven, or Himself.

Sickness Induction

On another occasion, while I was on disability, I was coming from the psychologist when I noticed a young black woman who just sat in front of me on the train. The Holy Spirit alerted me to keep my eyes on her.

Soon, the young woman reached into her handbag and took out something. She put it between her legs and started to squeeze tightly on it. She started whispering intensely as she continued to squeeze on the thing. Later at home, I realized that I was bleeding lightly and recognized that the young lady was trying to induce sickness on me. Thank God it did not happen as intended.

The many spiritual incidents that happened to me on the train were not all evil intent. I thank God for the young girl He sent to warn me of things to come and the white man who helped to relieve me of some evil spirits.

Chapter 8

Spiritual Incidents at Work

After seeing that I was successfully conquering the evil spirits sent against me at home, the tactic of the person conducting such an anonymous crime changed. The attacks began to include my place of work.

Air Being Sucked Away

One day at work, I was sitting at my desk working on the computer when I felt as if the air around me got sucked away. I realized that I was under a different kind of evil spirit attack. I was feeling pressed down and suffocated. As I walked away from my desk, I could get normal air to breathe. I went to the bathroom and washed my face a couple of times. I knew that running water helped to deter some of them, in the past. That provided a little relief.

I decided to go to the vending machine in the cafeteria to get water to drink. I put my money in and pressed for water. No water came. I decided to get my money back but pressing the return button did not work. I looked to see what else in the machine I could buy for the same price, since there was no water. I pressed regular Coke. Although Coke was not my favorite, I decided to drink it because I didn't want to lose my money. To my surprise, I burped a little and find that it brought significant relief to the feeling of being pressed down and suffocated.

I went to the computer lab to continue my work there. After a while, the feeling of air being sucked away from the space around me, returned. I had to keep walking away from what I was doing to get air to breathe. I was in the lab when I got very upset as air got sucked away. I took out a few sheets of paper from my notebook and wrote the works, *"Back to Maggie Francis,"* until I filled up three sheets of paper. I then went and put it in my small Bible, at Psalm 91.

The problem with air being sucked away from in front of me, whenever I sat to work, continued throughout the day. I drank Coke throughout the day to get the little relief that it provided.

Due to the constant trips I have to make to the bathroom, I asked my manager to allow me to move to an empty cubicle that was next to the bathroom. I told him that

I had to use the bathroom often due to a medical condition. At first, he was hesitant but eventually he agreed to it.

That day, I bought Coke to take on the train with me so that I could sip it to get occasional relief. After I got off the train, I had to walk home, as usual. When I got near the house, I was drinking the Coke. I find myself spinning in a circle while I released Coke from the bottle to form a circle around me. I was not sure of the meaning of what I did, but I knew it had to do with keeping away evil spirits. The Holy Spirit had directed my action.

Venom Ingestion

One day after I moved to the new cubicle at work, I was sitting around the computer when in the corner of my eye I saw a shadow passed by. I turned to my right to see who it was.

As I turned I felt like a stream of something going through my mouth and down my throat. I started to feel pressed down in my chest. I knew that it was evil spirit that passed by and poured its venom down my throat.

Spiritual Interference in Performance Review

On the day of my performance review, I was in a room with my immediate supervisor and the manager. I knew that there was the strong presence of evil spirit in the room.

The manager was pointing out that my performance needed improving. I was agreeing to everything that he said because I just wanted him to hurry up and finish. I was feeling severely pressed down and suffocated because of the presence of evil spirit. The manager was recently transferred to my group and he was tasked to transform it to work to a different standard. I was running out of patience with his talking.

After the new manager joined the group within a few months I had gone on disability with my back problem. I had not returned too long prior to this performance evaluation. I was not fully recovered when I returned to work.

The new manager had given me a writing assignment. At times, I could not think clearly because of the oppressed feeling brought about by evil spirits.

I told the manager that my performance was not up to par because I was sick. The supervisor asked if there was anything she could do to help. I told her that I was dealing with it.

I started crying. That was the best thing I could have done. The manager did not linger much longer. I was very relieved to get out of that room. I was wondering if I was going to survive being in that room because of the strong pressed down and suffocated feeling I was having, due to the presence of evil spirit.

The performance review was on a Friday. Starting the next Monday, the manager was out for a few days with severe cold. I knew that it had to do with him being surrounded by evil spirit during the performance review. From my experiences, many times I had cold-like symptoms because of being in contract with evil spirits. They can cause slime-like deposits in the body and would, therefore, lead you to believe that you had a cold.

My Worst Valentine's Day

On Valentine's Day, Thursday, February 14, 2008 while at work, I was feeling severely pursued by evil spirits. Again, everywhere I went, it didn't take too long before the airspace around me seemed to get sucked away. I had to keep walking away from my work, which was not productive.

I had a late lunch that day. As I sat having my lunch in the cafeteria, the cashier came over to me with a raffle ticket and asked me if I recognized the phone extension and name on it. She had called the extension, but it was incorrect. The cafeteria staff had a special Valentine's Day raffle. The handwriting looked familiar to me. I recognized it as that of Sally, but strangely enough, she wrote her phone extension with two of the digits switched. I told the cashier the correct phone extension.

Later, Sally collected her prize of chocolate in a heart-shaped box and passed in the lab to show it off. I was in no mood to be appreciative of such things. I was much too pressed down and suffocated.

This was the day that I thought I would die. On my way home, while waiting on the train, God released a song from my CD that let me know that I would not die but live to do His works.

Chapter 9

Spiritual Incidents at Home

Most of the spiritual attacks I experienced occurred while I was at home. It started at my home with outright spiritual attacks in which the angels of God led my defense with Psalm 23 and Psalm 91. The detail of this is in chapter 4. After outright spiritual attack at my home, I sought refuge at my sister's home. However, her home turned out to be the battleground. The attacks I describe in this chapter all took place at her home.

Bathroom Incident and Anointing in the Shower

On one occasion, I decided that I would bring the CD player to the bathroom to listen to songs while I took a slow bath. I usually play my battle song, *Step on the Enemy* (Lang, n.d.), continuously throughout the day. However, this time, I felt like listening to some other song. I went downstairs and looked at the Gospel music collection. I came across one which had "*Broken Vessel*" written on it. I chose it since I recognized that it was my deceased sister's handwriting.

I started to play the CD while I filled the bath. I was stirring the bath to dissolve mineral salts when the song about Judas betraying Jesus, *Thirty Pieces of Silver*, started playing. My spirit called out, "*Shame on you Teddy Dakins. I never knew you would do something like that.*" I began to wonder why my spirit said that when he was not the one bombarding me with evil spirits. I also had another bathroom incident which involved anointing my The Holy Spirit.

One day, I meet a young girl on the train with a book. The title included "*Two Novels*" and as she was reading it I saw something in it about shower. The next day, I was in the bathroom taking a shower when I found myself singing repeatedly, "*We shall be changed. We shall be changed. We shall be changed from mortal to immortality in the twinkling of an eye.*"

My left hand went across my lower back and I started spinning around slowly, as I continued to sing. I could not remove my hand from across my back. The shower was still running. I let the water washed over my head. I then found myself being gently lowered until I was on my knees. My head then bowed. I was in a position of being anointed, much like what you would see when a queen, or king was anointing someone. I stayed like that for a few minutes as the water washed over me.

After a while, I was able to gently get up. I then heard myself saying, *"I am a killer in the name of Jesus. I kill demons in the name of Jesus."* I have heard of and experienced being anointed by the Holy Spirit, through another human being. However, this anointing was performed directly by the Holy Spirit – without a human between.

Exercising the Anointing

The day after the anointing in the shower, I found out why I had spoken that I was a demon killer. I was attacked by evil spirits while in the bathroom and knew that they entered my body. I started saying, *"Get out in the name of Jesus. You are an idiot. I trap you and then kill you. Idiots, get out. You are messing with the wrong woman and the wrong family."* After repeating, *"Get out in the name of Jesus"* for a while, I find myself going down on my knees while saying it.

After I was in a bowed down position, I realized that the evil spirit was in conversation with Jesus. It was saying through me, "*Yes, yes. I will leave her alone; alright, alright.*" After the conversation was finished, I was able to get up.

Again, later in the same day, a similar attack occurred. I could not tell if it was the same evil spirit, or a different one. I only knew that I was being bombarded by one evil spirit after another. Again, this evil spirit had to bow down before Jesus, through me. This time, in addition to agreeing to something, in English language, the evil spirit spoke an unknown language, through me.

Attacked by Satan Himself

A few days after the anointing in the shower, I was taking a shower when I found myself singing nonstop, "*What more do you want Him to do? Jesus died on the cross to save us all. What more do you want Him to do?*" I wondered what was coming up next. The next day my daughter, Maud, called and said that her father asked her to pick up a document I had for him. I searched through the many documents I had taken from my house and found it.

After I found the document and held it in my hands, I could smell ants. I heard myself called out, "*Satan, Satan. I know it is you. Get out in the name of Jesus.*" I found myself bowing down on the floor. Next, there was a conversation between Satan and Jesus. Satan was agreeing to something, through me. After the conversation was over, I got up off my knees. I turned to a picture of Catreen in the room and said to it, "*No more madness in the family. I have conquered it.*"

I remembered the dream that I had of Catreen when she was showing me that she was not in her right mind. I could see that the individual who was sending all manner of evil spirits to me was trying to attack various parts of my body, including my mind. I was determined that she was not going to succeed.

I next found myself dancing and singing, "*Child of God, child of God, I am a child of God.*" I knew that the amazing rhythm I had when dancing was not normal for me. The moves were like what I saw in the Black History show with the sororities and fraternities. It also reminded me of the dream I had with God coming down from Heaven and dancing for a very long time as He quenched, with rain, many small fires that were springing up continuously (Reid 117-118).

After that victory, I was attacked twice by Satan and each time he had to bow down to God. Each time I danced and sang, "*I am a child of God.*" I even found myself doing the moonwalk dance that I saw the fraternities did in the

Black History show. The Holy Spirit was celebrating the victory over Satan, through me.

Attacks on My Eyes

I was attacked in my eyes many times. In these attacks, it felt as if a peck of dirt suddenly hit me in the eyes.

On one of my visits to the card reader she said she felt the eye attack sensation that I was having and commented about it. Before her comment, I did not explain that I was having such kind of attacks.

At home, I had to be constantly washing my eyes with eyewash while repeating, *"Go in the name of Jesus,"* until the spiritual darkness left my eyes.

The Use of Flies

Flies were used in spiritual attacks against me. In the heart of winter – January to February, my sister and I were seeing big flies in her house, which we didn't even see in past summers. They seemed to follow me wherever I go in her house.

While I was home on disability, one day the works of flies were more pronounced. I was getting ready to go to the doctor when two big flies came into the bathroom and pitched on the wall surrounding the bath. I took my slippers and killed one of them. Its blood was splattered on the wall. I cleaned it off.

I took a shower and then carried my coat downstairs to the kitchen area since I was getting something to eat. I put my coat on the dining room chair, which had nothing on it before. After I ate, I took up my coat to put it on. I noticed a big dead fly under my coat, even though there was nothing on the chair when I put my coat down.

I decided that I would get a glove to take up the dead fly. I went to the box of glove to get a glove and saw a big dead fly in the box. This indicated that whoever was hired to use spiritual means to cause me harm was trying all kinds of ways to drive me crazy. However, I was not afraid. I was not going to let anything they did drive me crazy.

I remembered the dream I had of *Catreen not being in her right mind* and that served as a constant determination not to let the works of satanic people drive me crazy. I knew that I was not only fighting for myself but also for my family.

When Catreen was in a similar situation and she was trying to tell some of her sisters that she was having problems with evil spirits they thought that she was crazy. One of them took her to the hospital where she was admitted to the mental ward. They did not think of other possibilities. Catreen got trapped in the mental health system and her life was never the same. I knew that she died so that she could help me, from the other side, to get through God's mission – a mission which involved fighting and conquering evil spirits.

Throughout my ordeals, I recognized that this was the mission which I dreamt God had for me. I had dreamt that, *I was telling my husband that God was ready for me to go on His mission, but it was as if he did not hear, or see me*(Reid). I left the house with a sense of determination and purpose. I turned on my CD to play the two songs of choice that I usually play as I walk to and from the subway and while on the trains.

Warnings of Upcoming Spiritual Attacks

God usually warns me of upcoming spiritual attacks before I face the reality of them.

One night I fell asleep and dreamt that, *I was standing at the door of a building, waiting for the doctor to come. I saw an endless line of chickens; pigs; women dressed in white, carrying black suitcases; and men dressed in white, also carrying black suitcases. I could not see the end of the line. As each animal, or human came* near me they disappeared to the right. I kept looking in the direction from which they were coming.

Before I could see the end of the line of the spirit forms of animals and human coming toward me, I woke up fighting an evil attack.

In another dream, God warned me about an upcoming spiritual serpent attack. Here is the dream. *My nephew, John, and I were in a building. We saw an injured serpent in a jar, packed with ice. There was a silver cross at the bottom of the jar. A lady standing by told us a few words that we should say. I then took the jar with the injuries serpent and walk through a door. As I passed through the door the serpent tried to lash out its fangs at me. I took the jar outside and poured out its contents near the bushes.*

The Spiritual Serpent Attack

The day after the dream about a serpent attacking me, I went into a room to get my clothes. As soon as I entered through the door, I felt as if something lashed me across my belly. It was more like a stinging sensation. I had a box with some of my documents from my house behind the door. I recalled the dream I had the night before about *the injured serpent in which it lashed out at me as I passed through a door.*

I decided that I was going to follow what I saw in the dream to get rid of the evil spirit that came in the form of a serpent. I went and bought a silver cross and put the cross at the bottom of a jar and then filled it with ice. I next took it to the room, read the 23rd Psalm, and then went and threw out the ice besides the fence.

I went back into the room and again had the sensation of being lashed across my belly as I walked through the door. I realized I did not say the words as the woman told us in the dream. It was just a few short words and not like reading an entire Psalm. I decided to repeat the process of putting the silver cross at the bottom of the jar and adding ice. This time after I placed the jar in the room I said, *"Go in the name of Jesus"* and then threw out the ice besides the fence. I went back into the room and did not feel any lashing sensation. This confirmed that I had said the right words to get rid of that evil serpent. Through a dream, God had given me the method of defeating the enemy.

The Divorce Attack

One night, as I lay in bed trying to sleep, I felt led to crunch down at the other side of the bed, as if trying to hide from someone. I then heard myself repeated two times, *"I will divorce Teddy Dakins."* I felt as if I was forced to say it.

Based on what happened, I realized that all the attacks I was going through was to separate my husband and me. My thinking was confirmed when I started the divorce process and as a result, spiritual attacks on me slowed down, drastically.

Jesus and God Are Fighting the Battle

I knew that God, Jesus, The Holy Spirit, and God's angels were helping me throughout my spiritual battles. However, one night I had a great experience of the entrance of Jesus and God into the battle.

That night, as I lay in bed trying to sleep, I find myself defending my mouth with my hand, repeating *"Jesus, Jesus, Jesus,"* as I came under attack by evil spirit. After a while, I stopped defending my mouth and heard myself spoke, *"Jesus is fighting for me."* I was overwhelmed with honor to know that Jesus was fighting for me.

I moved to the end of the bed and knelt for a few minutes before I went back to where I was lying down. I heard myself saying, *"Slaughter them Lord, slaughter them,"* repeatedly. After a while, I said, *"Jesus is fighting for me in the pit of Hell."* I next began to say, *"Strengthen Him Lord, strengthen Him."* After a while, I started saying, *"Slaughter them Lord, slaughter them,"* repeatedly, as if aware that Jesus got stronger. I then heard myself declared, *"Jesus conquered them."*

After that attack was over, I was able to relax for about fifteen minutes before I came under another attack. I was defending my mouth saying, *"God, God, God,"* repeatedly. After a while, I did not feel the need to defend myself. I started to shiver. I heard myself said, *"I am trembling at the throne of God."* I continued to shiver for about ten minutes.

The next day, as usual, I told Ruth about what happened that night. Both of us was shocked when we went to church later and the pastor, while delivering the sermon, said the exact words, *"Jesus went to the pit of Hell to fight for you."* I knew that God was confirming that both Jesus and Himself were fighting evil spirits for me that night and that my spirit was present at His throne. I hung my head in tears when I came to such a realization. Psalm 91 was song at church, which also confirmed by its words that Jesus and God fought for me.

Spiritual Sexual Attack

I am not sure what is achieved by spiritual sexual assault, but it seems to be used to accomplish devious things.

One evening as I was having my bath I find myself declaring, "*Blood of Jesus, blood of Jesus, blood of Jesus all over, blood of Jesus inside out*," repeatedly as I wash myself from head to toe with the bath water. The next day, I was in the bathroom downstairs when I suffered a sexual spiritual assault. I found myself crying out for Jesus.

After it was over I knew that attack was revenge for declaring the blood of Jesus all over and that the intention was to disrespect Jesus. During the day, two other similar attacks occurred. When I went to church the following Sunday, the lesson read was about the woman of Samaria. The pastor while preaching said that the woman of Samaria was called to be an apostle of Christ and had to do shameful things in the name of Jesus. Once again, I realized that God was confirming what happened to me with the spiritual sexual attack in which I had to suffer such indignity in the name of Jesus.

The Spirit of Discernment

Before I started to discern evil spirits that are on others, God allowed me to fight an attack that called out the spirit of discernment.

One night when I was under attack, I heard myself repeating, "*Spirit of discernment,*" while defending my mouth. The next Sunday when I went to church I saw the dark shadow of evil above the heads of a Black woman and two White males inside the church. With this incident, God demonstrated that He had given me the Spirit of discernment.

Spiritual Incidents on the Internet

It might seem strange to say that evil activities can be transmitted across the phone. However, this is my experience, only while talking to my husband on the phone. I started to refuse his phone calls and because of this he started sending me emails.

One day, I clicked to open one of my husband's emails. I got a spiritual pushing away sensation, like been pushed back by the wind. I quickly closed his email and stopped opening his emails. This was like what happened when I had clicked on a voodoo link on the internet to get information to help understand what was happening to me.

I had suspected that someone was using voodoo against me. Like the voodoo link situation, God was preventing me from communicating with him because of what was going on with me, spiritually.

The Warning Not to Let Him in Is Heeded

I experienced the reality of the death warning by the angelic young girl, on the train, with the Cosmopolitan magazine. One day while I was home, the doorbell rang. I started going to the door to open it when I feel a very strong spiritual pushing away sensation. I heard my husband called out to me to open the door, saying he wanted to talk to me. I told him that I could not talk to him and walked away.

At that moment, I remembered the young girl on the train with the Cosmopolitan magazine having a story about someone familiar that a woman let in and then got killed by him. The strong spiritual pushing sensation was a warning to me not to let my husband in. The pushing away sensation I got was an indication that evil spirits had followed him. These evil spirits intended to kill me. I thank God for warning me before I was faced with the situation. His warning allowed me to foil the plot of the enemy against my life.

Chapter 10

Day of the Lamb of God

God demonstrated to me that this chapter is very important to Him. He directed me to have a woman, who is a member of my church, do the final edits on my manuscripts, starting with the one for this book. After the woman finished editing the manuscript, she kept forgetting to bring it to church to give to me. God fixed it such that on November 24, 2013, the incorporation anniversary of His Company, Works Of Trinity, LLC, the woman finally remembered to bring the manuscript to church and she gave it to me, before the service started.

That Sunday, God also lead the moderator of the service to call on me to read Revelation chapter 5. I very rarely get called on to read the scripture at church. Revelation chapter 5 is about the seven seals on a book in Heaven. I started reading from verse 1. As I reached verse 2, tears started flowing from my eyes and became more intense as I continued reading. I was struggling to continue reading. When I reached verse 4, I started crying outright, in my spirit, with groaning. My head went down on the Bible, which I was reading, and I continued to cry in my spirit. The woman that had edited my manuscript came to the podium with her Bible and placed her hand on me as she finished reading the scripture, for me.

God had started my tears to flow until I reached the main part of the scripture which He wanted to demonstrate and then the Holy Spirit within me took over the crying. Here are the verses where the Holy Spirit started demonstrating the scripture. *"And I wept much, because no man was found worthy to open and to read the book, neither to look thereon. And one of the elders saith unto me. Weep not: behold, the Lion of the tribe of Judah, the Root of David, hath prevailed to open the book and to lose the seven seals thereof* (Revelation 5:4-5). Other verses speak of the Lamb that was slain and how worthy He is to take the book and open its seals. He is worthy to receive power, riches, wisdom, strength, honor, glory, and blessing (Revelation 5:6-13).

I knew that my faithful God was acknowledging my obedience of establishing a company for Him and of writing books, as Jesus had asked me to do. I further showed obedience to God by allowing the woman at church to edit my manuscripts, after He told me to do so, in a dream. The demonstration of the scripture reading revealed to me that Jesus has opened the special book in Heaven and is losing its seven seals. It also reminded me of the title of this chapter, *Day of the Lamb Of God*. This chapter title was chosen because of the spiritual incident with the intolerable smell of burning lamb which drove me to go to the hospital.

How It All Started

On February 24, 2008, I was upstairs at Ruth's house. She was downstairs working on the computer. I kept hearing a beeping sound as if coming from the entrance door in the hallway. After a while, I decided that it had been going on long enough. I went and told Ruth that something was wrong with the door, since the alarm kept beeping. She said that the door was probably not closed properly. I went and made sure that the door was closed properly. However, the beeping continued. I went and told Ruth that the door was closed, but the beeping was still occurring.

Ruth finally decided to come upstairs and check for herself. As soon as she came upstairs she recognized that the sound was the fire alarm from her tenant's apartment, upstairs. She said, "*Sandy must have something burning on the stove.*" She rushed and got the key for upstairs. I was right behind her as she opened the door to the upstairs. We were greeted with thick white smoke on the stairs but did not see any fire. I told her to call 911. She turned back and called. I told her to wet a towel and use it to cover her face. I wet a white towel and cover my head, nose, and mouth. Ruth went up the stairs and I followed behind her. She went directly to the stove and found a pot with food burning. She quickly turned off the stove. Luckily, no fire had started but the entire apartment was filled with smoke and had a very strong smell of roasted lamb, or goat.

Although I had the towel over my head and nose, I found the smell to be intolerable. Ruth started to open the windows. Just then the Fire Fighters arrived. She explained to them that her tenant left food on the stove and that it was burning, but there was no fire. Sandy arrived in the middle of all the chaos. When she realized what she had done, she was extremely upset with herself, saying, *"In 35 years I have never left food on the stove. I don't know why I did this."* She tried running up the stairs to see the extent of the damage. I held on to her and brought her outside.

While I held onto Sandy, I prayed to God to take charge of the situation. I thought that the situation was the work of Satan to get at me. I felt that whoever was working evil against me wanted to smoke me out of the house. That night, Ruth insisted that Sandy slept with us to avoid the smoke situation upstairs. It was rough for me with the smell of burning lamb, or goat. All the time, I kept the damp towel on my head and over my nose. I decided to damp the towel with salt water to protect my head since I was told that taking salt water bath helps to reduce the power of evil spirits.

I went to bed with the damp towel over my head and with a shower cap over it. I felt strongly that I should protect my head because I thought that evil was trying to mess with my head. I was determined not to allow them to conquer.

I could not sleep that night. In the morning, after Ruth, Berta, and Sandy left; I lay in the bed trying to fall asleep but couldn't. The alarm from upstairs started going off about thirty minutes after Sandy left. I called Ruth and told her about the alarm. I told her that I would go to Sandy's apartment to check if she had closed the windows. Ruth said that the Fire Fighters should have taken down the alarms, but I should go and check to make sure.

I went to Sandy's apartment with the damp towel still on my head and wrapped across my nose and mouth. I saw that the windows were still opened but one alarm was left in place. I called and told Ruth that one alarm was still in place. She said it must be the carbon monoxide detector. I tried going back to sleep but the alarm kept going off and the smell was becoming overpowering.

I found myself constantly singing in my mind, "*Lamb of God, sweet Lamb of God. I love the Holy Lamb of God.*" I went with very little sleep for close to two months and without any sleep, for a few days. I began to feel a kind of haze in my head as when you are out in the sun for too long. I realized that this was the sensation that Catreen had allowed me to feel when I dreamt that, *she was not in her right mind*. I was determined not to let them drive me crazy. I could see that the individual who was using evil spirit to injury me was doing everything to get her way.

Time to Depart

I made the decision that I had to leave the house before the smell of burning lamb overpowered me completely. I took a quick shower and packed my Bible and a few overnight clothes in a red bag. I remembered that the card reader had given me a clear liquid and said I should damp a towel with it and put over my eyes while I slept. I should then ask God to show me who was doing things to me. It had always been a problem to remember to do this. However, this time,

I strongly felt that I must find out who was doing things to me.

Before leaving the house, I decided to damp two sheets of paper towels with the liquid, laid down, and then asked God to show me the one who was sending evil spirits to me. I lay on my back and tried to concentrate. I found myself repeating, *"Body, mind, and soul must align."* I found my hands stretching out with palms up, my head moved slightly from one side to the other then back in the middle. My legs positioned themselves together and slightly bent. I realized that the position I was in was typical of pictures of the crucifixion of Christ. To add to that, I had the towel on my head, which was typical of what men, wore in Christ's days.

I must pause here to share a spiritual incident which occurred during the final revision of this book. When I read the above paragraph about me being positioned as depicted by the crucifixion of Christ, I suddenly remembered the two pictures I had from my trip to Israel in November 2016. They are ancient carvings of Jesus Christ, as a Black man, on the cross. These pictures were taken at The Church of Nativity in Bethlehem. I knew that these statues were extremely important to God. I was not able to take pictures of them because my phone ran out of memory. I just got pictures of the statues about a month ago, from someone who was also on the trip. I know that I have been through some very rough spiritual experiences with me being attacked by evil spirits while being helped by God, Jesus, and The Holy Spirit to overcome them all. Many times, the situations are confusing; I just tell my stories truthfully, even when I do not understand them.

Now…back to the crucifixion positioning of my body. After I felt released from that body position, I realized that the trials and tribulations I was going through must somehow relate to Christ dying on the cross. I rechecked the bag that I packed and decided that I should carry the damp towel, in a plastic bag, and a few other items. I finished packing what I needed to stay a day or two somewhere else. It seemed that returning to my house would be better for a while because there should be less evil there.

I cleaned up the room. By the time I got things together, it was late evening. My jacket was soaked with evil from Friday 15, 2008. However, I had to wear it since it was very cold outside. I decided to leave by the side door. After walking around to the side of the house, I see Ruth and Berta opening the front door. Ruth asked me where I was going. I told her that I just could not stay because of the smell of burning lamb and that I was thinking of staying the night at my house. I could see that Ruth was looking helpless. She asked me to call my friend, Donna. I told her I would and started walking to the subway.

Chapter 11

Hospital Experience

I was smoked out of Ruth's house by the burning smell of lamb. Therefore, I started on a journey that I thought would lead to my house.

Emergency Hospitalization Directed by the Holy Spirit

While walking to the subway, I came across a scene where an old woman was in the process of being placed in an ambulance. My spirit alerted me to this and I started thinking that this was probably what my enemies wanted to happen to me.

I called my friend, Donna. I told her about the problem with the smoke situation at Ruth's house and the burning smell of lamb that I could not tolerate. I told her that I was on my way to my house to get some relief from being constantly pursued by evil spirits. She told me that the Holy Spirit told her to take me to the emergency room.

Hospital Experience

She was still at work, so she asked her brother-in-law to pick me up and take me to his house where she would come and get me.

After Donna came to her sister's house, she got her friend, Pastor Rickets, to drop us at the emergency room on February 25, 2008. I felt like a battle-worn soldier. For the past few days, I did not sleep but was going through continuous spiritual attacks. Donna told me to tell the doctor about the incidents of evil spirits on the bus so that they would give me psychotic medication. In this encounter with evil spirits, I could hear the conversation among a few people, being directed at my circumstances. Donna told me that the individual who was sending all those evil spirits to inflict injuries on me wanted me to go mad.

Not to Be Dissuaded from My Destiny

While I was at the hospital, the card reader who had helped me, previously, called and told me not let them put me in the hospital because they were going to say that I was mad. I told her that at that point I did not care because I was very tired and badly in needed rest.

My niece, Alma, also called me. I also told her that I badly needed rest because I had no sleep whatsoever for a few consecutive days. I was willing to stay in the hospital to get the rest I badly needed. I was feeling thoroughly soaked with evil spirits, pressed down, and suffocated.

I knew that my jacket was also soaked with evil spirits. While I was in the waiting room of the hospital, I handed it to Donna to keep while I sat away from her. She was not aware of the presence of evil spirits on my jacket because they were targeted, or assigned to do me harm, no one else.

The Admission Process

When I was able to speak to the attending psychiatric, I deliberately focused on telling him that I was having constant nightmares about evil spirits attacking me; that I overcame them by calling on Jesus; and that there was an incident on the bus in which people was talking about my life. I told him that I was desperately in need of rest.

I was admitted and put in a very small room that was well ventilated. I could feel the relief as there was an excellent constant venting of air. The pressed down, suffocated feeling started to ease as I sat in that room. I took a shower and then decided to braid my hair in three. As I did the braids, I repeated, *"Father, Son, and Holy Ghost."* While I was braiding my hair, the attending nurse and the attending psychiatric came in to ask more questions. They gave me medication and after I answered their questions, they left.

When I finished braiding my hair, I was passing the lounge area to get to the bathroom when I heard one of the staff said that the air conditioning was down. I knew right away that the evil spirits had created that situation since the ventilation system was relieving me of some of their effects.

After I went back into the room, the pressed down and suffocating feeling began to return since the fresh circulation of air was no longer taking place. I tried to lie down and sleep, but it was difficult. Again, the attending psychiatric came in and told me that another psychiatric wanted to talk to me. I went and told that one the same thing I told the attending psychiatric.

I went back to the room and before long the attending psychiatric came to me again. I got angry with him and told him that I needed to sleep, and he was constantly interrupting me. He told me that they could not admit me to that hospital because they did not participate in my insurance. He was looking for a hospital to which to transfer me. After a while he came back to tell me that they found a hospital in Manhattan, which participated in my insurance; they would be transferring me to that hospital since they could only keep me overnight.

Later, I was yet again interrupted and was told that I had to do a brain scan to check for chemical imbalance. I went to do the test and was told that there was no sign of chemical imbalance. I went back into the room and tried to sleep. I must have taken a nap. I was not sure. I had no sense of time. The nurse came to inform me that the ambulance was ready for me and they had to take my blood pressure.

After my blood pressure was taken I was told that it was slightly high. They decided to wait a while and take it again since with my situation with the admission process and everything else it was reasonable for my pressure to be slightly high. After they took my pressure again, it wasn't much lower, but they decided that it was OK to transfer me.

My Journey to the Next Hospital

I was placed on a stretcher and taken to the ambulance outside. Another work of the enemy was that another ambulance was parked in the way, preventing the ambulance I was in from leaving. I heard the ambulance driver complaining to his assistant that the other ambulance driver should never have blocked the exit and that it was very unusual.

The ambulance I was in had to wait a while. It gave the evil spirits time to catch up with me. After lying in the ambulance waiting, the feeling of being pressed down and suffocated started to increase. I was relieved when the ambulance eventually started to move.

Admission and Orientation

I arrived at the Gracie Square Hospital in the night and was placed on a stretcher and wheeled in. As I entered a passage way, closed to the admission area, it was quite warm, and I had increased pressed down and suffocated feeling. I could sense that the presence of evil spirits was strong in this area. There were stretchers lined up one behind the other for admission. After I got out of the passage way, I was relieved. However, as the door from the passageway opened to the admission area I could feel a draft of the spiritually foul air.

After I was processed, I was taken to the floor that I would be staying and then to my room. There were three beds in the room; one was already occupied by a woman who was sleeping. The nurse's aide got me fresh pillows and blankets. He then took me around to show me the area and explain how things operated there. He took me to the dining area.

As I entered, I saw a group of people sitting around a table. I saw the dark veil of evil spirits over their heads. The nurse's aide introduced me to the group of people. A guy said to me, *"Welcome to Hell."* The nurse's aide gave me a snack from the refrigerator and then took me back to my room. I settled down to try and get some sleep.

I was awakened by another patient who was being assigned to the room. I did not sleep much because that woman was constantly groaning. I could tell that that woman was plagued by evil spirits. I placed my pillows in the sign of the cross and laid on them.

The next day, I introduced myself to the roommate who was there before me. She was a recovering alcoholic. I found out that I was on the floor with people recovering from drugs and alcohol problems. The next day I was relieved to find that they transferred the constantly groaning roommate to the psychiatric floor.

I decided to read my Bible. I felt that I should read about Jesus, so I flipped the pages to the New Testament. I opened to Mark chapter 3 and was immediately drawn to the following passage, *"No man can enter into a strong man's house, and spoil his goods, except he will first bind the strong man; and then he will spoil his house"* (Mark 3:27). You have to bind the strongman in his house before you can plunder it. I thought, *"If this is Hell, as the man commented, then I am in Hell to bind and conquer Satan."* I knew that I was directed by Jesus Christ to that scripture for a reason.

The New Roommate

Two nights after the groaning roommate left, another one came. It was a young girl who attempted suicide. She got the bed that the former groaning roommate occupied.

That night as the new roommate was putting away her clothing, I was semi-asleep. I could see through my spiritual eyes, a constant stream of darkness leaving me and going into her clothing bag. I felt much lighter, that is, much less pressed down and suffocated.

In the next few days I came to realize that the evil spirits that left me had somehow become attached to some of my new roommate's clothing. After she changed her clothing I could feel the penetrating feeling of evil spirits when I was close to her. I persuaded her to wash her clothing. I showed her the washing machine and helped her to get her clothes washed. I also cleaned her closet for her.

New Patient and Activities

A few days after handling the new roommate-clothing situation, an elderly lady came. I could tell that evil spirits were surrounding her. She quickly told everyone that she was an Opera singer. At times, I would be sitting close to her and feel the sensation of evil spirit coming from her.

I had to attend special group meetings including Alcohol Anonymous (AA) and participate in activity sessions, such as Bingo and Arts and Craft. In one of the AA meetings, my spirit was moved when one drug-addicted veteran spoke that he was *"sick and tired of being sick and tired."*

In another AA meeting, the Opera singer was talking, and my spirit started urging me silently, *"Don't listen, don't listen,"* repeatedly. However, I heard some of what she was talking about. It had to do with someone working witchcraft and her children being gay. This caused her to lose her mind when she found out.

While I was in the hospital, my sisters, Petra and Ruth, came to visit me one day. Another time my nephew, Paul, came to visit and once Donna came to visit me, by surprise. I spent about three weeks in the hospital. When it was OK for me to leave the hospital, Paul came to pick me up and he took me to Ruth's house.

Chapter 12

Post-Hospital Experiences

While in the hospital, I had decided that my enemy would not stop bombarding me with evil spirits until I divorce my husband. After I left the hospital, within a few days I went to see a lawyer to start my divorce process. After that, the attacks slowed down, drastically. I guess the individual working to cause me harm had some satisfaction that I had to go into the hospital and that I started the divorce process.

I knew that the individual must be spending a lot of money to afford such constant bombardment of evil spirits. All efforts with the use of burning candles and using bath liquids from the card reader, who I saw a couple times, seemed useless considering such constant bombardment of evil spirits. It was only the constant help of God that saved me. He didn't have to go and buy ingredients to put together a defense. He knew what He was dealing with and how to deal with it, instantly. After all, He is the head of all principalities and power (Colossians 2:10).

Baptism

Long before I came under severe spiritual attacks, I was seeking to be water baptized. Two pastors from different churches had turned down my request because they said I would first have to attend baptismal classes. At that time, I was going to a different church where water baptism was not done by submersion, as I desired.

A few weeks after I left the hospital, I met someone, who I had not seen for many years. He was bishop of a church near where I was living. I visited the church and asked him if he could baptize me whenever his church was having baptism. He agreed.

The Friday night before the baptism, I was attacked in my groin area. I defended myself saying, *"Nothing can stop me from serving God."* I was baptized the Sunday, along with a man and another woman.

New Attacks

I started the divorce process. However, it was demanding of information and very expensive. Soon, my deposit ran out and I started to get additional bills for the service. My husband was also feeling the financial burden of the divorce. We eventually met to discuss the divorce and I agreed to withdraw it.

I soon realized that my act of withdrawing the divorce proceeding resulted in new spiritual attacks. This time, it seemed to be coming from a different person. This was confirmed in church when the bishop got a revelation while he was praying. The Holy Spirit revealed to him that someone was using evil spirits to try to cause my death, like how my sister died. I recognized who this new person was. However, I was reluctant to believe it.

Spiritually Fed with Evil Venom

One day, Teddy asked me to pick him up from the airport. As I got close to the airport he called me to say that the plane had landed. While speaking to him on the phone I felt the force of something seeping through my mouth and down my throat. I quickly told him that I was on my way and hung up the phone. I could tell that it was an attacked of evil spirit, which was sending something down my throat.

I didn't say much to Teddy on the way to our house. I dropped him at our house and went back to my sister's house, even though it was late at night. I began to wonder about the source of the attack I had while speaking to him on the phone. The day after I picked up Teddy from the airport, the tenant upstairs complained that she was attacked by evil spirit in the form of a man. She believed that it came in with me when I came in late that night since it happened after she heard me come through the door. That evening my sister, Ruth, called my friend, Donna, and spoke to her about me being attacked by evil spirit after picking up Teddy from the airport.

While Donna was on the phone, the Holy Spirit revealed to her what had happened. Someone had consulted with an Obeah worker to do harm against us. Ruth handed the phone to me and as Donna continued speaking, the Holy Spirit took control of her. She started speaking in tongues. She later told me that her belly was heaving constantly as she spiritually pulled whatever entered my body when I went to pick up Teddy at the airport.

Breaking Away from Card Reader

The realization of who might now be doing something to harm me spiritually was very disappointing to me. I went back to the card reader to find out what she could tell me. She confirmed that it was the same person, revealed by the

Holy Spirit to Donna. I asked her to help prevent these new attacks.

She told me to come back for liquid bath and candles. Later that night, I spoke to Donna and she told me that the Holy Spirit told her to tell me not to mix human work with God's work. God will take care of the person because He had the higher power. I went back to the card reader since she was expecting me. I took what she gave me, but after I got home, I decided that that was my final visit to her. I threw out all the liquid bath, candles, and beads to carry in my purse which should keep away evil spirits from me.

I finally concluded that I must rely on God alone as my defense; since when I looked back, it was only through His might that I was able to overcome all the different types of evil that came against me. I was not able to prove if any of what the card reader did helped, since I was being constantly attacked anyway. God was always there in exactly the moment I needed Him to defend me. He always knew exactly which evil spirit is attacking me and how to counteract it.

Chapter 13

An Extraordinary Life

In a fairly short period of time, I had been experiencing some extraordinary spiritual events in my life. Since I had very little background in spirituality, I mostly did not understand what I was going through, and not sure how things came about. However, I did recognize that it was a fierce battle between God and the kingdom of darkness, with me been in the middle of it. I had been through so many kinds of spiritual attacks that I thought I had experienced them all. I was mistaken about this.

Another round of very serious continuous attacks started in January 2010. I am happy to say that although the form of evil was much fiercer – demonic in nature, I did not go back to the card reader. I stood up to evil spirits and demons using the all-powerful words and spiritual movements of God, which His Holy Spirit gave me, "on time." This time, the attacks were less frequent and, therefore, I had time to record them exactly as they occurred. I refer to these attacks as incidents since they are all awakening experiences.

There are a few exceptions where the incidents are not spiritual attacks. The incidents happened for a reason. God pointed out that my life was meant to be extraordinary.

(Incidents: Spiritual Gunshot, 1/5/2010)

I noticed a big fly buzzing around the light in the bathroom as I prepared to take a shower. I remembered previous attacks where flies were used. However, I dismissed this one.

That night, I was asleep when I heard a very loud noise close to me. I woke up with my heart beating rapidly. I looked to my right, in the direction where the sound came from. I saw that the closet door was wide open. It was shut before I went to bed and to open it, one would have to pull very hard since it usually closes tightly. I was sleeping with my daughter, Kristal, in the room.

The next morning, I asked Kristal if she heard the noise last night. She told me that, *she was dreaming of hearing a gunshot and that there were two suspicious people trying to come into the house. She told Ruth not to let them in.* I realized that this was an evil attack, designed to generate a heart attack, by spiritual gunshot.

(Incident, Jesus' Request to Write Book, 1/8/2010 to 1/10/2010)

On Friday, January 8, 2010, I started a three-day fast. At the end of the fast, Sunday, January 10, 2010, I dreamt that, *I was in a room. There were a few books on the bed. I moved my hands over the books and called my daughter's name, Sonia. I started saying the word, "book," repeatedly.*

I woke up saying the word, "*book.*" I could not stop myself from repeating the word, continuously. After a very long time, I hear myself spoke out, "*Jesus, I will write you your book.*" After I spoke these words, I became aware, in my spirit, that I was having a conversation with Jesus. It was as if I was listening to instructions and acknowledging them. This went on for quite some time. I could mostly hear myself saying, "*eehi*" – indicating "*yes.*"

While my spirit was in communion, my mind recognized that my spirit was speaking to Jesus and urged my spirit to ask Him when I was going back to my house and to ask about my husband. My spirit ignored my mind.

(Incidents: Jesus Is Calling Ruth, 1/11/2010)

I was at the dining room table, reading. I had my netbook computer opened. My spirit got moved to continuously sing part of a song, "*Jesus is calling, calling, calling.*" My sister, Ruth, and daughter, Kristal, were upstairs. I was there singing for quite a while – maybe twenty minutes. There was no way I could see who was coming down the stairs, but as soon as I heard footsteps, my spirit cried out, "*Jesus is calling Ruth.*"

Next, my head went down on the netbook computer. I knew that whoever came down the stairs was in the dining area. My spirit started a conversation with Jesus. It continued for quite some time. I was only acknowledging what I was being told. After a while, I heard Ruth said, "*What are they revealing to you?*" My spirit continued to commune with Jesus and ignored her. She got impatient and came around to me. She held on to me and said, "*Cut it out. It doesn't do any good if you can't interpret it.*"

At that point, I started to bawl out [cry out loud] in agony as if mourning for someone who died. Ruth panicked and called my friend, Donna, to tell her that I was crying out. Ruth thought that my bawling out was caused by evil spirits since I was constantly under attack by them. Donna response was that I should take my medicine. I told both Ruth and Donna that I could differentiate evil spirit from that of Jesus' because His Spirit doesn't hurt your body.

That night I dreamt that, *my medication fell on the floor. They were broken up and the floor was dirty. I picked up the pieces and tried to paste them together. They turned white and wet instead of being burgundy. I was thinking that they were no longer good. Ruth passed by me. I asked her to give me a plastic bag in which to put the medication.*

In the morning, I decided to start taking my medication, although I did not see the need to do so. I took one pill and put it on a piece of white tissue while I brush my teeth in the bathroom. After I finished brushing my teeth, I looked for the pill to take it. I did not see it. I looked on the floor and saw that it had fallen to the ground, just as I had dreamt. I believed this incident was confirmation that I did not need to be taking the medication constantly. I knew for sure that I needed it when I was suffering from severe lack of sleep and mental exhaustion.

I was not taking the medication for over a year even though I have been through extreme mental challenges while working on a project that was severely behind. I wasn't getting much rest but was able to get a tremendous amount of work accomplished, without taking any medication. God allowed such challenges to prove it was mental exhaustion, brought on by constant spiritual attacks, which resulted in the need for medication. There was an opportunity to be laid off while the company was cutting back on staff, but God allowed me to be transferred to a new group to face such a challenge.

The next morning Ruth told me that she came under attack by evil spirit. The shadow of darkness came upon her in her sleep and she had to cry out, "*Get out in the name of Jesus.*" The evil spirit had come to kill her. I realized that I was mourning in my spirit for Ruth because of what would later happen to her. The ways of the spirit are strange to the natural man and will cause unnecessary concerns. This was the case when I was mourning in my spirit, loudly, for Ruth.

The time has come for us to embrace the ways of the spirit as being beyond the comprehension of the natural man. For some whose spirits are awakened, the natural minds are not in alignment with the spirits and hence there will be the sense of abnormality. In fact, if the natural man could understand the spiritual man, it would be quite normal to him.

A few days later Ruth dreamt that, *she was back home, in Jamaica, directing people as to how to rebuild the old church that we used to attend.* Her dream confirmed that Jesus was calling her to do work, as was revealed to my spirit that Jesus was calling Ruth. You just never know the way you will be called to do God's work. However, the enemy always shows up to challenge your calling; as was the case with Ruth.

(Incidents: Evil Birds Took Flight, 1/23/2010)

I wanted to go to the Rite Aide pharmacy, which was about ten minutes' walk from where I was staying. Outside, I debated whether I should walk or drive because I was feeling lazy. I finally decided to walk because the temperature was mild.

On my way back from the pharmacy, I walked on the opposite side of the road. One block away from the house, I happened to look across the street. I noticed a house with the statues of two birds. I thought to myself, *"There is something significant about those birds."*

Later at home, Kristal asked me to drop her at the subway station, since she was running late for work. After I dropped her off on Green Street, I made a left turn onto 233rd St. A car was driving ahead of me. However, although the car just drove on a part of the road and I was close behind it, suddenly, two white birds appeared on the road in front of my car and flew over it. This reminded me of the two statues of white birds I saw at the gate of a house, earlier in the day.

Later that evening, Dr. Bishop Hutchinson, whose church I would attend occasionally, decided to visit us after promising to do so for quite a long time. When he came, my sister, Ruth, was not here. I called Ruth to let her know that he was at her house. While we were waiting for Ruth, I told him about some of the spiritual battles I had been through with evil spirits. I told him how we used the *"Step on the Enemy"* song by Christopher Laing (Laing, n.d.) as one of our weapons in the battles and played it continuously, on auto-repeat. I told him the story of how the Holy Spirit instructed my friend, Donna, to give me her CD and told her to play that song and another one *"Obeah Woman Yu Power Catch Cold."* I could hardly believe when he told me that he knew Christopher Laing, personally, and that he would sing at his church, sometimes.

It was getting late, so I called Ruth once again to find out when she would arrive. She told me to ask Dr. Bishop Hutchinson to pray until she comes. However, Dr. Bishop Hutchinson decided to wait on her. After Ruth came, they chit chatted for a while then we decided that Dr. Bishop Hutchinson should pray. Ruth suggested that we hold hands in a circle.

Dr. Bishop Hutchinson requested that we moved the circle to around Ruth's living room table. Ruth's friend, Harry, was with her and so he joined us in prayer. Dr. Bishop Hutchinson prayed and before the prayer ended, he said that a white bird, which was at the table, flew away while he was praying. It was an evil spirit and God had directed him to form a circle around the table, as he prayed. The evil spirit could not tolerate the prayer and, so it left. I then told everybody about my experiences of noticing the statues of two white birds and then seeing two white birds flew over my car. Apparently, those white birds that flew over my car were evil spirits and one of them had followed me into the house.

(Incidents: Cleansing with Strawberries, 1/26/2010)

I woke and used the bathroom. I find that the CD which was set to continuously play my battle song, "*Step on the Enemy*" had stopped. "*No*" was on the display. I tried restarting the CD but was unsuccessful. I was lying awake for some time when I find myself saying "*Jesus conquers*" and at the same time I was defending my entire belly with my right hand. This continued for about fifteen minutes.

After that, I did not go back to sleep. The alarm went off to get up for work. When I went to the kitchen, Ruth was preparing her lunch. She asked if I also wanted to take lunch to work. I told her that we were having a Department meeting in the morning and there would be food, so I would only take fruits and have fruits for the rest of the day.

At work, just before lunch, my friend, Donna, called me and asked me to check an email she sent me. Just before I decided to check the email, I decided to eat the strawberries that I had brought with me. I was eating while checking my email. As I opened the email, my eyes landed on an email from my daughter, Maud. It had the subject containing fruit. Since I was eating fruit at that moment, I decided to open that email first. I read about the benefits of eating fruits on an empty stomach and of the superb antioxidant property of strawberries. The literature also suggested going on a fruit cleansing diet for three days. I remembered that my belly was spiritually attacked that morning.

On my way home, I stopped at the fruit store and bought a lot of strawberries to go on a three days strawberry cleansing diet. It occurred to me that God had directed me to cleanse myself with strawberries. It was not a coincident that Donna called me and I decided to check my email while eating strawberries, only to see an email that caught my attention, which had information about eating strawberries to cleanse your body. I needed to cleanse my body after last night's spiritual attack.

(Incident: Spirit Flavored Tea, 1/28/2010 to 1/29/2010)

While at work, I decided to drink some Bigelow green tea. The tea had the flavor of goat, so I decided to stop drinking it. This was not the case before, since I had tea from that pack before. I knew that it was evil spirits messing with my food.

In another incident, on January 29, 2010, while at work, I decided to drink some tea and bought Mint tea from the cafeteria. While I was drinking it, I had the faint taste of ant. I thought that it must be due to the sugar. I drank all the tea.

After I went back to my desk, I decided to use the phone. I got a faint smell of ant from the phone. I knew then that something was terribly wrong, since this reminded me of the other times when ants were used in evil attacks against me. I had my CD with me with some Christian songs, so I decided to put it on repeat and keep the volume very low. After a while, I began to feel as if ants were crawling on top of my head.

(Incident: Satan Has No Power, 1/28/2010)

In the evening while I was reading the prayers in *"God's Creative Power..."* book, I realized that evil spirits had penetrated my body. As I read, *"I am the body of Christ and Satan hath no power over me. For I overcome evil with good"* (Capps 18), my spirit took over as I repeated those words. I next heard myself saying, *"No power,"* repeatedly.

The evil spirit within me reacted, eventually; it spoke through me as it started to cry out, saying, *"Oh no, oh no."* repeatedly. After that reaction was over, I continued reading more prayers.

My spirit reacted to the following prayer, *"I don't desire to eat so much I become overweight. I present my body to God, my body is the temple of the Holy Ghost, which dwelleth in me. I am not my own, I am bought with a price, therefore, in the name of Jesus I refuse to over-eat. Body settle down, in the name of Jesus and conform to the Word of God. I mortify the desires of this body and command it to come into line with the Word of God"* (Capps 21). My spirit took over and I find myself repeating the words, *"conform to the Word of God"* in a loud commanding voice.

My spirit also reacted to the following prayer, *"I am a believer and these signs do follow me. In the name of Jesus, I cast out demons, I speak with new tongues. I lay hands on the sick and they do recover"* (Capps 28). I find myself repeating, *"In the name of Jesus I cast out demons."* The demons reacted through me as I heard myself groaning and saying, *"Oh... Oh...,"* repeatedly.

My spirit reacted to the following, *"Jesus gave me the authority to use His name. And that which I bind on earth is bound in Heaven. And that which I loose on earth is loosed in Heaven. Therefore, in the name of the Lord Jesus Christ, I bind the principalities, the powers, the rulers of the darkness of this world. I bind and cast down spiritual wickedness in high places and render them harmless and ineffective against me in the name of Jesus"* (Capps 28). I find myself repeating, *"That which I loose on earth is loosed in Heaven."*

After a while, the evil spirits within me reacted. I started blowing out my breath while I said, *"loose,"* repeatedly. This continued for a while.

I reread the prayer. My spirit reacted again. I heard myself repeating, *"Render them harmless and ineffective against me in the name of Jesus."* I knew that evil spirits were present in my body because I occasionally felt like ants were crawling on top of my head. This feeling continued up to the next day.

(Incidents: The Good Luck Kiss, 1/29/2010)

On October 5, 2009, I was transferred to a new group on my job. A week before I was transferred to the group I dreamt that, *I was in a room, sitting down. My co-worker, Sally, came to me and said, "Good luck in your new job." She then kissed me very hard on my mouth. I could feel the effect of the kiss throughout my body. It was not a good feeling. She then gave me two transparent plastic bottles of clear liquid. They were about 2 ft. tall. One was half-full while the other was full.*

The next day I told Sally about the dream. The day I started work in the new group, I had the flu. It lasted for about two weeks with the worst part being experienced in the first week. The feeling of the flu reminded me of the feeling in the dream and it was all over my body. That first week I sent an email to Sally to let her know how I was doing since we were now in separate locations. I did not hear from her for about a week, which was unusual.

When I heard from Sally, she said that she was out sick for a week. I did not question what was wrong with her since I knew that she had sarcoidosis disease and sometimes she was out, sick, because of it. Two months after leaving my former group, the group had a reunion. I was able to see Sally again. I mentioned to her how I started the new job being sick. She then told me that she too was sick that same week with the flu. We both marvel at the coincident that we were both sick at the same time when I started my new job. We remembered the dream I had with her kissing me and giving me a terrible feeling throughout my body.

(Incidents: Too Close for Comfort, 1/29/2010)

A few days after I met Janet, a member of the new group, I started feeling suffocated and having clogged ears whenever I was around her. The feeling reminded me of my previous experiences with evil spirits. I knew something was wrong. Shortly after I joined the group, my friend, Donna, had dreamt that, *she saw a woman very close to me at my job and she was wondering why she was so very close.*

In January 2010, at work, I was assigned a project with Janet as my mentor. Before this, I would avoid contact with her whenever I could, so that I wouldn't get the feeling of suffocation around her. With that assignment, I would have to be in close contact with her, constantly. The week of January 25, 2010 we started working close to together, often, which caused increased exposure to what was on her that would cause me to feel suffocated. I tried to manage the best I could. However, I started praying desperately to God to show me what was wrong with her.

On January 29, 2010, in the morning when I was working with Janet, the suffocating sensation from her was very strong. I started praying desperately to God to remove the spirit from around her. After lunch when we had to resume working, she came back to my desk without a sweater. I no longer got the suffocating sensation around her. I knew the spirit was attached to her sweater.

(Incidents: Power of God Defense, 1/30/2010)

I took a shower and went to the boiler room to put away my clothes. As I opened the door, it seemed as if something was preventing it from opening completely. I could get inside the boiler room, but I needed to get in more fully to hang my clothes. I looked up and did not see anything blocking the door. I looked down and saw a foot of water boot blocking the door. I wondered if this was an act of evil spirit since it was not normal to be there and earlier in the day, my sister, Ruth, had seen one of those big flies that typically would come around before an attack. I dismissed the idea of the boot been there by an act of evil. I picked up the boot and placed it somewhere else.

I went back upstairs and washed my hands. I took out my prayer book and started saying the prayers. I was still on the first prayer when I find myself wiping my face with my right hand – the one I used to pick up the water boot. I knew that I was under attack and that the boot in the boiler room was the trap.

The intensity of the face wiping action increased. Next, I found myself struggling to say the words, *"power of God"* while I continued wiping my face. After a while, I stopped wiping my face. I used my left hand that had the little book as well as the right hand to cover my face completely and started saying, "God, God, God..." repeatedly for a long time. Next, I started saying, *"kill them God, kill them,"* repeatedly for a while. Next, with both hands still covering my face, I started shaking my head while repeating the same words. Next, I started shaking my upper body while repeating the same words. After this, the shaking was of my lower body and then my legs. It slowed down after a while. I repeated the word, *"Teddy Dakins,*

Judas," many times. I stopped after a while and was able to remove my hands from my face.

I started re-reading the prayer book. After a few prayers, I found myself blowing out air from within me, repeatedly. Towards the end, my tongue curled within my mouth as I blew out the air. I realized that demons were trying to dry out my mouth so that I could not speak out as I read the words of God. I forced myself to stop and then continued reading the prayer book.

(Incidents: The Use of Psalm 91 and Hymn 221 In Spiritual Battle against Ant Evil, 2/1/2010)

In the morning, I was free from the feeling of ants crawling in my head. At work, I decided to have some nuts to eat. After I started chewing on some of them, I got the faint taste of ants. I decided to stop eating. I started feeling as if ants were crawling in my head, once again. I realized that once again, evil spirit got into my food.

I remembered that in the morning, before I left the house, I had noticed two ants crawling on the floor near the bag, which I usually carried to work. The situation with the taste of ants in the nuts reminded me of the ants crawling away from the bag. I realized that God allowed me to go to the bag that was related to work so that I could see the ant and quickly make the connection to what I was experiencing. This prevented me from eating all the nuts. It was very unusual to see ants crawling around at that time of the year.

When I got home, as I walked down the stairs to go to the dining area, I got a faint smell of ants. I remembered what happened to me at work with ants and food. I realized that evil spirits were in the house.

I decided to get my Bible and read Psalm 91 in every room of the house. I started upstairs. After doing two rooms and the bathroom I went to the living room and opened the entrance door, which was close to the outside door. I started reading Psalm 91. After a while, the tone of my voice changed drastically, more like that of a man. My voice got louder as I continued the reading. I was aware that my daughter, Kristal, came from the room to find out what was happening. The tenant upstairs, Sandy, came down to find out what was happening. I continued my reading without acknowledging them.

After a while, I started repeating verses 10 and 11, "There shall no evil befall thee, neither shall any plague come nigh thy dwelling. For he shall give his angels charge over thee to keep thee in all thy ways." I find myself jumping around while I read.

My sister, Ruth, was downstairs and came up to find out what was happening. She held onto me and said I had to try to keep it down because there were people downstairs. At that time, the boiler repairman was fixing the boiler. My spirit continued in a lower tone, but not even Ruth could stop me.

Ruth told me that I have to tell them to, *"Leave NOW in Jesus name"* and to *"Go to a dry place until Jesus comes"* (according to what Dr. Bishop Hutchinson told us the night before). I was able to do as Ruth instructed. I made sure that I opened the outside door as I was commanding the evil spirits to leave.

After I was done, Ruth, Kristal, Sandy, and I started discussing spiritual experiences, theirs as well as mine. Sandy said to me, *"Doesn't he know that it is going right back to him?"* I knew who she was talking about. I asked her, *"How many people must tell me that?"* My spirit then reacted and called on Jesus to send it back now, saying, *"Send it back now Lord, send it back now,"* several times.

Later, Kristal told me that what was happening to me was not normal, because not only did my tone of voice changed to that of a man, while reading Psalm 91, but also my face was angry. I knew that it had to be the evil spirit in me because evil spirits hate the words of God.

I decided I also needed to incorporate Halleluiah praises in the battle against the evil spirits that were attacking me. Yesterday, Dr. Bishop Hutchinson told Ruth and me about Halleluiah being the highest praise and that he had told his congregation to give God six Halleluiah praises, six times, for six days. Because of this, I decided to find the Halleluiah song that came to my head while I was bathing. This was, *"The strife is o'er, the battle done... Alleluia [Halleluiah]."* I had my very old Presbyterian Hymnal but could not find it in the index since that page was missing. I was determined to find that song, so I leafed through the Hymnal until I found it as # 122.

Later that evening, I read Psalm 91 and I did my prayers from the prayer book. After the prayers, I sang the Halleluiah Hymn. At verse 4 and onwards the tone of the singing changed as if in a man's voice. I repeated the first verse. After I was done singing, I started to say, *"Thank You..."* for quite a while. Afterwards, I felt as if I was listening to someone. I knew it was Jesus. I sat in bed in that listening state for a while. During my battles with evil spirits, God, Jesus, and The Holy Spirit always show up in one way or the other to take me through what I was facing.

I went to bed lying on my back with my feet crossed and my hands crossed in an X over my heart. I lay awake for a while. After some time, I find my hands (still crossed) circling my heart. I started to say, *"Go now to a dry place and stay there until Jesus comes. Go now in the name of Jesus. You do not live here, Jenness, lives here,"* repeatedly. After a while the evil spirit in me responded and spoke through me, saying, *"Go now,"* repeatedly and then, *"dry land,"* repeatedly. Next, I started to blow from deep within me. This continued for a while until it gradually faded. I knew that this action was to get the evil spirit out.

(Incidents: Body of Christ, 2/2/2010)

I woke up and said my prayers before getting ready for work. I remembered that I had a book in the bag, which I regularly carried to work, but didn't yesterday. The day before, I had seen two ants crawling away from the bag, although you wouldn't normally see ants in the heart of winter. As I reached for the book in the bag, I got a faint smell of ant. I made the mistake of sniffing the bag to make sure. I decided that it smelled of ant.

Through the many evil attacks I experienced, I became familiar with the smell of ants being one form of the presence of evil; especially when the behavior was not in line with that of normal ants. Because I needed the book,

I took the book from the bag instead of carrying the bag with me.

While driving to work, I realized that I was contaminated with evil spirit. I started to use the same words as last night to get rid of the new evil spirit that got into me. After a while, the evil spirit reacted in a similar manner. As before, in the end I finished with blowing out air from deep within me. I opened the car window to allow the evil spirit to leave.

At work, I went to the cafeteria to get coffee. While at the coffee stand, two white men joined me. One was telling the other that he was supposed to have gotten married last Saturday but he broke it off. He said the woman was trying to take him as a slave to her and her kids. He said that after he realized this, he had to call off the wedding; it took him three months to do so. The other man asked how she was taking it. He said that she was calm. The other man said she might come back with a vengeance.

I paid for the coffee and went to the elevator. Soon after I got on the elevator, a woman and the same man with the broken engagement joined me. They were conversing. The man was directly in front of me. I noticed that he had a silver chain around his neck with a cross hanging from it.

Later at work, I was working at the computer when I get a faint smell of burning goatskin or lambskin. I found myself repeating under my breath, "*Body of Christ.*" It was difficult having to say this constantly while the attack was going on. I eventually pulled a sticky notepad and wrote on it, "*Body of Christ.*" I then proceeded to underline the words vigorously and forcefully for quite a while. After some time, I find myself very forcefully piercing the notepad with the pen, as if driving the nail through Jesus' hands.

After that attack subsided, in another fifteen to twenty minutes I was going through some documents related to the project I was working on when I started to get a very faint smell of ants. I was sitting at my desk working with documents on the computer as well as with printed documents around me. I could sense an attack, by evil spirit. I clenched my teeth together and opened my mouth very slightly. I started to say, "*Go now in the name of Jesus to a dry place and wait until Jesus come,*" repeatedly.

After a while, the evil spirit responded to my words in the usual fashion of repeating my words. I next blew the evil spirit out. At the end of blowing out, I started to think that my body was proud of my spirit due to the discrete way it was handling the attacks, at work. I later start to repeat in my mind, *"Body love spirit."* This was around 9:25 a.m. I drank some water to toast what I thought was the alignment of body and spirit. I kept praising God for the victory, quietly.

I went to the cafeteria to get a coke and hot water in my thermos. After I returned to my desk, Janet and Wane stopped by. While talking to Janet I got an extremely faint scent of ants. After Janet and Wane left, I started to rub my nose intensely as I got a strong smell of burning goat, or lamb meat. I felt like it was going to suffocate me. I was practically closing my nose and breathing through my mouth. After this attack was over, I decided that things were getting too intense and it could reach a point where I might be unable to control the situation. I sent email to my bosses and told them that I had to leave because of medical problem. As I passed by Razan's cube, I told him I was leaving because I wasn't feeling well.

In my hurry to leave, I left the Hymnal that I took to work. After I was far on the road, I remembered it. I decided that I would just go to a Christian bookstore to buy a new one. At the bookstore, I could not find the same kind of Hymnal. I decided to find a Hymnal that had the *"Halleluiah"* song in which I was interested. I searched a couple of hymnals and found the song in the Chalice

Hymnal. The interesting thing was that, the hymn number in this one is 221. I remembered that it is 122 in the Presbyterian Hymnal. The numbers were reversed. I knew that this was a sign that God would reverse the evil attacks on me, as I asked Him to.

I called my sister, Ruth, and told her about the reversed numbering of the hymn in the Chalice Hymnal. I also mentioned that with the first attack on the job, my body was very pleased with my spirit and declared that my body loved my spirit and that my body was aligned with my spirit. She said to me that it was usually the reverse. The spirit would declare alignment with the body.

When I went home, the kitchen area was soaked with the smell of ants. It was so strong that it was overpowering. The area of concentration was at the garbage can, close to the kitchen sink. I saw that in addition to ants crawling around, a piece of yam that Ruth had bought was almost completely covered with ants. In the heart of winter, you do not normally see ants. Such abundance of ants and their extremely strong smell indicated that an army of evil spirits had come to try to inflict harm on me.

I got my Bible and read Psalm 91 throughout the house. I then decided that I was going to face these evil spirits and try to get rid of them. In the kitchen area, I put on the battle song, "*Step on the Enemy*" (Lang, n.d.). I stayed in the dining/kitchen area commanding evil spirits to go to dry places and stay until Jesus comes. After a while, I held a bottle of water to my mouth for a long time while I was singing after the battle song.

Finally, I removed the bottle of water from my mouth. I started saying, "*Halleluiah*," repeated. I declared Halleluiah everywhere – on the food, all over. I commanded the evil spirits to say Halleluiah and praise the Lord. I knew that I was soaked with evil spirits. I had the strong stench of ants on me. When I was finished, I had to wash the clothes I was wearing. When going to bed I decided to open the Hymnal to #221 on my chest and go to sleep. I was anticipating an attack while sleeping. I slept, woke up to use the bathroom and went back to sleep without being attacked.

(Incidents: Message of Extraordinary Life, 2/3/2010)

While driving to work, I released evil spirits several times, by telling them to go to a dry place until Jesus comes and then blew them out. I knew that they were from the army of evil spirits in the form of ants that I had to deal with yesterday.

It was uneventful at work even thought I knew I did not get rid of all the evil spirits yet. I could still feel a few crawling on top of my head.

When I got home, my daughter, Kristal, asked me to follow her to church because she was concerned with my situation and wanted me to ask for prayer. I didn't want her to think that I was ignoring her concerns, so I decided to go with her. John Bevere DVD was shown, which was related to his book, *Extraordinary: The Life You're Meant To Live*.

I knew that God had me go there because John Bevere delivered many messages to me. John spoke about God rewarding you. As he spoke this, I remembered the meeting at work about being rewarded with pay increase for good works. I felt the messages many times in my spirit as he preached. John spoke of God rewarding you for good works; of the danger of deception by living a projected life; of you looking in the mirror and seeing yourself as you are; of God's plan for you to live an extraordinary life; etc. I certainly felt that my living had turned out to be extraordinary with the many encounters I was having with evil spirits. At the end of the session, I asked the pastor if they were out of the book in the bookstore, as he mentioned earlier. He gave me his own copy, which he was showing the congregation. I later realized that it was God Who prompted him to give me his copy of the book, because my life had indeed become extraordinary.

Chapter 14

Revelation of Anti-666

Before going into my stories of the revelation of the anti-666 Spirit, I must first present my research on the spirit of 666, which is described in the Bible. I found relevant information in Daniel chapter 7 and Revelation chapter 13.

Biblical Background on "the Mark of the Beast" - 666

Although Daniel chapter 7 did not mention the number 666, like what John, The Revelator, saw in the book of Revelation, Daniel had a vision of four beasts coming out of the sea. Three of the beasts are described by animal characteristics - lion, bear, and leopard. The fourth beast was dreadful, terrible, exceedingly strong, had great iron teeth; it devoured and broke in pieces and stamped the residue with its feet. It had little horns with eyes like a man, and a mouth speaking great things (Daniel 7:2-8). It would devour the whole earth and destroy it (Daniel 7:23). It would speak eloquently against the most High [God]; thinking to change times and laws, and to make the children of God weary. The child of God would suffer under this beast for *"a time and times and the dividing of time"* until the time of judgment when the children of God would take away the dominion of this beast; destroy the beast, get dominion of the kingdom under the entire Heaven, and all dominions would serve the most High God (Daniel 7:23-27).

Daniel saw that the beasts' thrones were destroyed; the Ancient of Days then appeared with clothing as white as snow and with the hair on His head looking like pure wool. Judgment was set, and the books were opened. The last beast was destroyed, while the other three lived for a while (Daniel 7:9-11). The Son of Man [Jesus Christ] was given everlasting dominion, glory, and a kingdom that all people, nations, and language should serve Him (Daniel 7:13-14). The four beasts are four kings on earth; but the saints of the most High will take away and possess the kingdom forever, even forever and ever (Daniel 7:17-18; 7:21-22).

John, The Revelator, described a single beast which is the composite of the beasts described by Daniel. It came from the sea. This beast took on three animal characteristics - a lion, a leopard, and a bear. It spoke great things and blasphemies; it blasphemed the name of God, His tabernacle, and them that dwell in Heaven. It was given power and authority by the dragon; had a deadly wound in one of its head, which caused the world to wonder about it. People worshiped the beast and the dragon which gave power to it. They expected that no one would be able to make war with it. Power was given to the beast to make war against the children of God and to overcome them. It was given power over all people, language, and nations; it would be able to continue this for 42 months. People whose names are not written in *The Lamb's Book of Life* would worship the beast (Revelation 13:1-8).

A second beast came from the earth. It had the animal characteristics of a lamb and a dragon. This beast had all the power of the first beast and caused the world to worship the first one, whose deadly wound was healed. The second beast would do great miracles and deceive many by this. It would request that an image of the first beast be made and that people should worship the image. The second beast had the power to give life to the image of the first so that the image would speak. People who would not worship the image of the beast would be killed. The second beast would cause people of all background to receive a mark in their right hand, or in their foreheads and no one would be able to buy or sell, unless he or she "had the mark, or the name of the beast, or the number of his name; the number of the beast is the number of a man; and his number is Six hundred threescore and six" (Revelation 13:11-18).

Both Daniel and John, The Revelator, described the 666 beast as symbolic of the world's political system which rules over all people, language, and nations (Daniel 7:17; 7:23; Revelation 13:7). This beast was given power by the dragon, which is otherwise called the Devil and Satan. The animal characteristics of the four beasts in Daniel chapter 7 are those of lion, bear, leopard, and one not named. In Revelation 13, the animal characteristics of the two beasts relevant to 666 are those of lion, bear, leopard, and lamb; and the dragon [Satan] is named as the one who gave power to the beast. This is not surprising to me since Satan has been deceiving people and creating untold havoc in their lives, after he was thrown out of Heaven and came to earth (Revelation 12:7-9).

Now that I have given background information on the 666 spirit, I will describe the incidents leading up to my encounter with it. I will also describe how I dealt with its attacks. This was by far my greatest struggle with evil forces and should not be taken lightly. I believe that The Holy Spirit chose to give me this revelation because the time of the *"mark of the beast"* (Revelation 16:2; 19:20; 20:4) is here. There are some spiritual incidents, which I believe were prelude to the 666 spirit revelation.

(Incidents: Walking with Jesus Wristband Exposed, 2/4/2010)

In the morning, on my way to work, I could tell that evil spirits were in the car with me. I had to get rid of them while driving – from my belly and elsewhere. I had to be crunching down, squeezing on my belly on the right side and telling the evil spirits to, *"Go now to a dry place and stay until Jesus come,"* over and over again until I got some relief. I also had to be blowing them out through my mouth. I was getting rid of evil spirits all the way to work.

After I parked the car, I picked up my book bag to take inside the building. My right thumb somehow moved to the horn and pressed hard on it. I took it as a warning not to carry the book bag with me. I took out a book I wanted to use during lunchtime. I left the bag in the car.

In the morning, I had to go to the bathroom about three times to get rid of evil spirits, using the name of

Jesus. After lunch, Janet came over to my desk to show me something. I felt the suffocating feeling that I experienced around her, previously. We went to speak to some co-workers and then returned to my desk. I did not realize that my *"Walking with Jesus"* wristband was showing, since I had on long sleeve shirt. Janet touched it and told me that she was also a believer.

While Janet was at my desk, our manager, Donna, stopped by to talk to Emon, whose cube was next to mine. Donna told Janet that she had a pretty angel on her sweater. She was wearing a well-decorated sweater and I did not notice the pin before. I believe that The Holy Spirit was showing me that she was one of His; even though I had the suffocating problem with her. I was not sure what issue she had that caused a spirit to be with her. I wondered if one of those evil spirits that were constantly after me was using her to get to me, since she was my mentor.

(Incident, The Two Black Birds – Carriers of Evil Spirit, 2/4/2010)

On my way home from work, while on the exit off the highway, two black birds flew over my car. My spirit alerted me to them. I heard myself said, *"My God, not again."* I remembered my previous experience with two birds, as evil spirits, and one had followed me home. Very soon, after the birds flew over the car, I felt as if I suddenly got a cut at the right side of my head. I use one of my right fingers to press tightly against the spot and kept on repeating, *"Blood of Jesus sanctifies."* All the way home, I drove with my left hand. I used my right hand to apply pressure to my head where I felt like I got a cut.

Soon after reaching home, I asked my daughter, Kristal, to check the spot at the side of my head and she said there was no cut. However, I could feel a small bump that was not here before. I decided to wash my hair, in the sink. In the process of doing, so I started getting rid of evil spirits one after the other while the pipe was running water. One evil spirit was trying to fool me as if it was gone when in fact it was still around. My spirit could sense this. I finally called, *"Power of God in me"* repeatedly, until I got rid of it.

(Incident, The Horse Demon, 2/4/2010)

After the hair washing drama in trying to get rid of evil spirits, I went around to every room in the house reading Psalm 91. From the first reading, at verse 9 with the words, *"The Lord is my habitation,"* I placed my right hand over my heart. I continued with my hand over my heart while I read the psalm, in every room. After I was finished, I placed the hymnal that was in the bag, besides me on the bed. I next said my prayers with my hand still covering my heart. While saying my prayers, I got the feeling of dust entering my nose. I could tell that it was from evil spirit that was in the bag since the hymnal was in it.

After the prayers, I went downstairs to use the kitchen pipe. I tried to get rid of the evil spirit that I knew I picked up from the dust entering my nose. It was extremely stubborn. About two months before this, I remembered a dream I had with dust getting into my nose at a building which I knew was a horse stable. In the dream, *I was standing outside the side door of a large rectangular-looking building. A black man was standing by the door. I knew there were horses inside the building. The man saw that I wanted to go inside the building through the door where he was standing. He motioned me to go towards the front of the building. I moved to the front of the building. There was a cloud of dust swirling around at the front. I could feel the dust getting into my nose. I put on a dust mask.*

Since I was feeling dust entering my nose, just as in the dream, my spirit started to call out repeatedly, *"Horse evil, giddy up and get out."* The evil spirit reacted. The running water did not bother this evil spirit as I had seen it done for others. Through me, the evil spirit acted as if it was drinking the water; this was unlike others I experienced, which did not like water. It used my legs to act as if it was doing *"giddy up"* as I had told it to do. I ranted and raged for this evil spirit to *"Go in Jesus name to a dry place...."* However, it was very stubborn.

My sister, Ruth, came home and wanted to use the sink. She gave me a towel to wrap my head and move to a chair to sit. I was still trying to get rid of what I thought was a horse evil spirit, while I sat in the chair. Ruth got angry and commanded the horse evil spirit to, *"Get out NOW in the name of Jesus."* It cried out through me and I fell to the ground making noises. Ruth opened the door and told me to get up and not to let it get me down. I got up and told her that I was going to put the bag in the gazebo since the evil spirit contaminated it. I knew that it had waited for me in the bag.

As I went outside, I noticed footprints in the form of hooves in some light snow that was in front of the gazebo. I put the bag in one of the chairs in the gazebo. I went inside and told Ruth about the hoof prints leading to the gazebo. She said they must be from a cat. I told her they were too big to be from a cat.

Ruth asked me how I handled situation at work. I told her about how I had to be getting rid of evil spirits while at work; about the suffocating problem I was having with Janet at work; and about what happened to me on the way home with the two birds. I mentioned to Ruth about the angel pin on Janet's sweater. I then started telling Ruth that Janet had told me that she was a believer when she saw my *"walking with Jesus"* wristband.

I looked at my right hand and there was no wristband. I knew that the evil spirit had taken it. Since a pastor at the church I was visiting put the wristband on my hand, I never took it off. It was a completely round plastic wristband and could not come off unless someone deliberately took it off. The evil spirit probably thought that the wristband was protecting me. I realized that The Holy Spirit had allowed Janet to comment on the wristband so that by relating this story to Ruth, I would realize that it was taken away from me.

Later, I drew a picture of the hoof print. The front of the hoof was about 4 ½" to 5" wide with a split in the middle. The back of the hoof was about 2 ½" wide with also a split in the middle.

(Incidents: Revelation of 666 and Anti-666, 2/5/2010)

In the morning, I continued my fasting by reading my prayers. I felt a little crawling around my nose. I forgot that I had the new hymnal from the bag, which was contaminated by evil spirit. It was on one side of the bed. I decided to smell some Florida water, which my sister, Ruth, had given me the night before. The horse evil spirit reacted to it, through me, as if the Florida water was irritating it. Seeing this, I started to use more and more of the Florida water as it continued to react. I started calling out for it to, *"Leave NOW in the name of Jesus."* This horse evil spirit was very powerful and kept on resisting.

Ruth came into the room and I asked her to pour some of the Florida water over my head. She did so as I continue to call on Jesus and call on God, trying to send the horse evil spirit away. It continued to resist but was still upset about the Florida water. I put some of the water in my mouth and started swirling it around. The evils – horse and whichever else, were reacting to this. I called upon the Almighty God to destroy them, as I continued swirling the water in my mouth.

I moved to the bathroom and started running some water. I put fresh water in my mouth and started swirling it around while I looked in the mirror. I could see how my face got distorted as evil spirits reacted to my efforts to get rid of them. I started rubbing one eye then the other as I realized that evil spirit was in both. I tried to get rid of them by telling them to go in the name of Jesus.

After a while, I stopped washed the bed sheets. I knew that the dust, carried around by the horse evil spirit, was still on them. After I started the washing machine, I decided to cut a stem of the aloe plant by the kitchen window and make tea to drink. My spirit spoke to the evil spirits, saying, *"I will let you drink the bitter cup of salvation."*

After cutting the aloe and putting it on the stove to boil, I started washing my hair. While washing my hair I let the water run over the spot that was still sore from yesterday, due to the evil attack in the form of two birds. I started to speak out, *"The name of Jesus is mighty,"* repeatedly. I then heard myself saying, *"He rose from the dead on the third day,"* repeatedly. Next, I started to say, *"Jesus is mine,"* repeatedly. Next, I started to say, *"666 go now,"* repeatedly. Next, I started to say, *"333 is mine,"* repeatedly. Next, I started to say, *"Jesus, God, Holy Ghost,"* repeatedly. Next, I started to say, *"Holy Ghost,"* repeatedly. Next, I started to say, *"Holy,"* repeatedly. Next,

I started to say, "*I am Holy*," repeatedly. After this drama, I realized that "*333*" was given to me by The Holy Ghost [Spirit] to counteract "*666*."

After the revelation of the anti-666, I went upstairs. My daughter, Kristal, came home after a while. She was surprised to see me at home. I explained to her what happened. She told me to listen to some Gospel songs. I had my battle song on while I was reading so I did not care to hear anything else. She insisted and turned off the CD player, which was playing my battle song. She turned on the computer and started songs from a website. The second song had a verse that repeated the word "*Holy*." My spirit was moved since it was confirmation of what I was saying earlier. I was repeating the word, "*Holy*" while fighting evil spirits. The Holy Spirit had used Kristal to give me confirmation of His work in helping to defend me against evil spirits.

The revelation of 666 reminded me of a dream I had in October of 2009. In the early morning, I dreamt that, *I was hearing the news on the radio that the ratings of President Obama dropped to 50 percent. I then saw President Obama carrying a long chain with a cross at the end. It reminded me of chain with cross that Catholic Priests usually carry.*

President Obama came to me as I was lying on my back. He used the cross to make a mark on my forehead and then put something around my neck. After he left, I looked and saw a ¼ inch black leather hanging like a necklace around my neck.

This dream also reminded me of the incident yesterday in which my rubber wristband was taken off my hand by what I thought was a horse evil spirit. During the incident, it had thrown me to the floor. The wristband was ¼ inch in size. The dream depicted President Obama to indicate the level of authority of this very stubborn evil spirit, which turned out to be that 666 demon and not a horse evil spirit, as I had thought. In October 2009, I told my co-worker, Sally, about this dream about President Obama. Her immediate reaction was, *"I hope it was not 666 he marked on your forehead."* I remembered her comment after the 666 demon was revealed.

(Incidents: Eye Evil Trapped in the Wrong Body, 2/5/2010)

While dealing with the 666 demon, I also had to deal with other evil spirits. During the day, I decided I could not go to work due to the many evil attacks I was experiencing. After the 666 demon incident, I decided to read John

Bevere's book, *Extraordinary: The Life You're Meant to Live*. The evil spirit in my eyes (eye evil) reacted to parts of the reading, acting shocked and curious as I read, *"A book was written about you...Your story is a book, too, and the Author is none other than God. He wrote the book before you were conceived in your mother's womb...God has designed accomplishments for you in your book...God has set goals for you"* (Bevere 21). As I read the following passage, the eye evil acted upset, *"For we are God's [own] handiwork (His workmanship), created in Christ Jesus, [born anew] that we may do those good works which God predestined (planned beforehand) for us [taking paths which He prepared ahead of time]"* (Bevere 21).

Later in the evening, I decided to end my six days fast with my prayers. I usually use the prayers from Charles Capps' book, *God's Creative Power Will Work For You*, as well as a few I wrote for myself. I decided to start with the prayers written by me. The eye evil spirit reacted to two of them. I asked God to, *"Give me the power that I need to overcome all forms of evil."* The eye evil spirit was upset and shocked and started to whimper. I wrote down the reaction of the eye evil spirit beside the prayer. After I wrote it, the eye evil spirit spoke through me asking, *"What now?"* I continued to read my personal prayers. As I prayed, "*Give me the power that I need to speak only words from You,*" the eye evil spirit reacted, saying, through me, "*What is this? Words from God?*" It then started to say, "*Oh no,*" repeatedly. Then it started to say, "*Let me go,*" repeatedly. I was not in a hurry to let this one go. I wanted to finish my prayers.

I next turned to the other prayers from Charles Capps' book. The eye evil spirit reacted to a few of the prayers. I read, "*I mortify the desires of this body and command it to come into line with the Word of God*" (Capps 21). Where I read, "*Command it to come into line with the Word of God,*" the eye evil spirit reacted, saying, "*Oh God,*" repeatedly. I continued reading. While reading, "*Transformed by the renewing of my mind*" (Capps 25), the eye evil, repeated these words in a very curious and questioning tone. When I read, "*My mind is renewed by the Word of God,*" (Capps 25), the eye evil became upset when I read, "*Word of God.*"

As I read, "*Jesus gave me the authority to use His name*" (Capps 28), the eye evil spirit was very upset and started to blow hard to show the extent of its anger. As I continued with, "*And that which I bind on earth is bound in Heaven. And that which I loose on earth is loose in Heaven*" (Capps 28), the eye evil spirit started whimpering, saying, "*Oh,*" repeatedly. The eye evil spirit was upset throughout the rest of this prayer, which read, "*Therefore in the name of the Lord Jesus Christ I bind the principalities, the powers, the rulers of the darkness of this world. I bind and cast down spiritual wickedness in high places and render them harmless and ineffective against me in the name of Jesus*" (Capps 28).

I continued to the next prayer. I read, "*I am complete in Him who is the head of all principality and power. For I am His workmanship, created in Christ Jesus unto good works which God has before ordained that I should walk therein*" (Capps 28). As I read the words, "*head of all principality and power,*" the eye evil spirit became more upset. After I said the words, "*good works,*" the eye evil spirit repeated these words several times and then asked, "*I have to do good works?*"

I got out my netbook computer and started to type, "*I can tell that the eye evil is very uncomfortable in this body. It should get out immediately.*" As I typed the first sentence, the eye evil spirit reacted through me. I looked up and threw my head back while crying out, "*Oh,*" repeatedly. After I returned to my typing, I made sure that I repeated the words, "*eye evil*" several times because those words upset it. There were no further reactions.

After my prayers, I went downstairs to the kitchen and put some food to cook. I decided to go back upstairs and continue reading John Bevere's book, *Extraordinary: The Life You're Meant to Live*, while I waited on the food to cook. I got reactions from the eye evil spirit as I read certain words. When I read, *"My life is not my own; it belongs to my Lord, Jesus Christ"* (Bevere 33), the eye evil spirit reacted with a sound indicating curiosity at the words, *"Lord, Jesus Christ."* At the reading of the words, *"...we offer people the blessings of resurrection power..."* (Bevere 33), I got a curious reaction from the eye evil from the words, *"resurrection power"* (Bevere33).

As I read, *"For the word of God is full of living power and resurrection power"* (Bevere 33), the eye evil spirit reacted with curiosity, as previously done. The reading of the words, *"It is sharper than the sharpest knife, cutting deep into our innermost thoughts and desires. It exposes us for what we really are"* (Bevere 33); caused the eye evil spirit to groan as if it was hurt.

As I read the words, *"If not, are we hearing the true Word of God?"* (Bevere 34); the words, *"true Word of God"* caused the eye evil spirit to stare severely, through me. As I read, *"Who among you truly fears God?"* (Bevere 34), the words, *"truly fears God,"* caused the eye evil spirit to purse my mouth and steer. As I read, *"Proverbs clearly shows that focusing on our projected image is a trap, and you won't know you're in it until it is too late"* (Bevere 34); the words, *"you won't know you're in it until it is too late,"* (Bevere 34) caused the eye evil spirit to cry out, *"Oh God Almighty,"* repeatedly. Then it started saying, *"Get me out,"* repeatedly; *"God Almighty, get me out,"* repeatedly.

At this point, I went back to the kitchen to check on the pot. The eye evil spirit continued to call on God Almighty to get it out. I moved from the stove to the outside door and opened it slightly while the eye evil spirit continued to cry out to God Almighty to get it out. After a while, it started saying word I used previously to get out other evil spirits. It said, *"Go to dry place."* Then it started saying, *"Out,"* repeatedly. I decided to open the outside door wider. Just as I did that, I saw a black cat, about one foot tall, ran across the lawn. The eye evil spirit continued to say, *"Out"* for a few more minutes; followed by blowing out; and then it was gone. This eye evil spirit certainly did not like the body it entered. It became entrapped and fought hard for its freedom. The Words of God were indeed cutting through it like the sharpest knife ever.

(Incidents: Identity of 666 Animal Form Revealed, 2/5/2010)

Later in the day, Dr. Bishop Hutchinson stopped by to pray for me. My niece, Rose, had called him to come and see me. After he came through the door, he put his hand on my head. I then told him about the incident with the evil birds and me driving home with one hand due to them attacking me. He walked me to the passageway and then handed me a small bottle with lavender oil. He told me that God directed him to give it to me and said I should use it to put a cross on my forehead. I then told him the Obama dream with the cross and the mark he made on my forehead. I thought, *"Dr. Bishop Hutchinson represented President Obama in the dream in which the president put a mark on my forehead, with a cross."*

Dr. Bishop Hutchinson told me he came late because he was praying at church to prepare himself. He carried his video camera that I had called and asked him to bring, so that he could film the hoof prints in the snow. I told him about the *"walking with Jesus"* wristband that was taken off my hand by what I thought was a horse evil spirit.

I took Dr. Bishop Hutchinson to see the hoof prints made by the horse evil spirit in the snow, but when we went outside the snow had already melted. I took him to the gazebo where the book bag was left overnight, and we prayed there. We went back to the dining area. There, he told me that God revealed to him that the evil spirit was a rhinoceros. He said the rhinoceros was one of those spirits that was very difficult to get rid of. My spirit reacted, and I cried out, "*I needed the name.*" Dr. Bishop Hutchinson said, "*Yes. When you call their names they will go because they do not like that.*" He then prayed for me.

My spirit reacted in a manner similar to the morning when I was washing my hair and got the revelation of anti-666. I was ranting and raging against the 666 demon to leave. Kristal came downstairs when she heard the commotion. I moved into the bathroom and started running water from the pipe while I continued to try to get rid of the evil spirit. I rebuked 666, declared 333, etc. Before going to bed, I wrote out a list of words I could possibly use to fight this rhinoceros evil spirit. I had mistakenly believed it was a horse evil spirit. The 666 demon was operating in disguise.

In the night, I woke up fighting evil spirits. I had both hands covering my nose and mouth with just enough space for me to speak. I tried using the words, "*Rhinoceros evil, unassigned Jenness Reid. Go now to a dry place and wait till Jesus come,*" repeatedly; "*Rhinoceros evil, you do not live here, Jenness Reid lives here. Go now in the name of Jesus," repeatedly; "Rhinoceros dust," repeatedly; "Rhinoceros evil, unassigned Jenness Reid, 333" repeatedly; at this point, the rhinoceros evil spirit responded, "Rhinoceros evil? Rhinoceros evil? I am a rhinoceros demon." It then started saying, "Go to a dry place?" repeatedly; "Name of Jesus?" repeatedly; "Unassigned" repeatedly.

My spirit took over and I started saying, "Rhinoceros demon, unassign Jenness Reid, 333, 333, 333, God, Jesus, Holy Ghost," repeatedly. The rhinoceros demon responded, "I did not know you have all three. Let me out, let me out, let me out." I responded, "Released," repeatedly. The rhinoceros demon started groaning while my mouth was closed, until it was released.

I concluded that the following words were key to the rhinoceros demon begging to be released: "Rhinoceros demon, unassigned Jenness Reid, 333, 333, 333, God, Jesus, Holy Ghost," repeatedly. I also concluded that calling a demon "evil" which is below its rank was insulting and, therefore, its pride allowed it to correct me. Using the correct name with the correct title along with, unassigned <your name>, 333, 333, 333, God, Jesus, Holy

Ghost, will allow you to get rid of the *"mark of the beast"* – 666, which has the animal form of a rhinoceros.

The anti-666, 333, was an extremely powerful revelation that The Holy Spirit allowed me to have, so that I can inform others that, while struggling with the *"bitter cup of salvation"* in the form of spiritual attacks and especially with that of the *"mark of the beast,"* they have a way out. The way out is to repent of your sins and seek salvation by asking Jesus Christ to come into your heart and be your Lord and Savior. Next, you repeat the following declaration: *"Rhinoceros demon, unassigned <insert your name>, 333, 333, 333, God, Jesus, Holy Ghost [Spirit]."* Holy Spirit can be substituted for Holy Ghost since it means the same. The anti-666 is 333. God allowed me to go through such traumatic experience, so that others can be helped when going through similar experiences.

After the revelation of the *"mark of the beast"* and how to counteract that demon, I wondered if there was connection with two incidents that occurred months before I encountered it. One evening, Kristal brought home an article that was circulating at her job. It was about an identification system which uses a FDA approved passive microchip as an insert in a person's body to link them to their personal health record, in case they go to the emergency room and are not able to communicate.

In less than two weeks after receiving this information from Kristal, I had to participate in a mandatory online employee verification process at a government website. I also wondered about this verification system. Could verification systems lead to the *"mark of the beast?"* After all, during the time of spiritual battle with the 666 demon, that was first masking itself as a horse spirit; I had a dream about President Obama making a mark on my forehead, with a cross. Later, I had the incident with the rhinoceros demon removing my symbol of *"walking with Jesus,"* from my right hand. In addition, there is the Biblical link of *"mark in the forehead"* and *"mark in the right hand"* to the *"mark of the beast"* (Revelation 14:11).

(Incidents: Walking with Jesus Wristband Returned, 2/6/2010)

After breakfast, I walked to the store and bought some sage, lavender oil, frankincense, and myrrh. I walked home. When I was close to crossing over from the opposite side of the road to my block, I happened to look down and saw the imprint of paws on the pavement. It shaped like that of a cat but was much bigger, more like that of a lion's. The track of the paws indicated that the animal crossed the road to my block.

On my block, I decided to take two cases of water from my car trunk, which I kept forgetting about. I was having difficulty with the two cases of water and the opened car trunk. A man passing by the side of the road I was on said, *"It seems as if you need help. Can I close your car trunk for you?"* I answered," *Yes.*" He asked if he could carry one of the cases of water. Again, I answered, *"Yes."* He said, *"OK. I don't like to ask because most people don't like when strangers help."* He left the case of water at the top of the steps. I thanked him.

While opening the door I started to repeat, *"333, 333, 333, God, Jesus, Holy Ghost."* I opened the second door and placed the cases of water just inside of the door with my right hand without entering. My handbag and the bag with the incenses were across my left shoulder all this time. I hesitated to enter the living room. I started saying, *"Holy Ghost,"* repeatedly. After a few minutes, I closed the doors to the living room and went outside. As I was on the step outside, the sage from the bag started to smell very strongly; this was unusual. I find myself marching to the gazebo where I had left my book, which was contaminated with evil spirits. All this time, the very strong smell of the sage fragrance followed me. In the gazebo, I rested the bag of fragrances beside the book bag and marched back to the front door. As I entered the living room, I started saying *"Holy, Holy, Holy,"* repeatedly, while I turned around many times.

Ruth was not home. After telling her friend about the spiritual attacks, her friend had advised her to wipe the house with vinegar and water as well as lavender disinfectant for areas close to the outside doors. Ruth called and asked me to wipe the house.

While I was wiping downstairs, Ruth came home. I was about to wipe beside the toilet bowl when I noticed my missing *"Walking with Jesus"* wristband, lying on the floor. Earlier that day, I had cleaned the toilet and the same spot on the floor, but there was no wristband there. I called Ruth and showed the wristband to her. I did not touch it. Later Ruth removed it and put it in the garbage outside. The rhinoceros demon had taken the wristband away but after its defeat, the lion (symbolic of Jesus Christ, Revelation 5:5) returned it. Therefore, The Holy Spirit allowed me to see wet paw prints of a lion crossing the road.

Chapter 15

It Is Not Over

After I dealt with the 666 demon and overcame it, I thought that was the end of my struggles with evil spirits. Unfortunately, I was mistaken. This chapter takes you through some additional spiritual incidents, after I thought that the battle with evil spirits was over.

(Incidents: Cursed Off by a Demon, 2/6/2010)

I was cleaning the bathroom. I finished the bathtub and was at the cabinet in front of the mirror. Suddenly I clenched my buttocks and lips. I started saying, with my mouth closed, *"Go now, in the name of Jesus to a dry place,"* repeatedly; *"Go now, you are unassigned from Jenness Reid, go now in the name of God, in the name of Jesus, in the name of the Holy Ghost, 333, 333, 333."* The demon responded, making crying sounds for a few minutes.

After the demon quieted down I continued, *"Go now, you are unassigned from Jenness Reid, go now in the* name *of God, in the name of Jesus, in the name of the Holy Ghost, 333, 333, 333; never to return, never to return,"* repeatedly. The demon reacted, saying, *"Unassigned, unassigned, never to return, never to return."* Then, very angrily it said, *"I am going, I am going; guwey, guwey."* It continued, *"Who want you anyway; move off, move off, move, move, boo, boo, boo, me gahne, me gahne."* The demon was making face at me while it cursed me. It then left. All this time I could see myself in the mirror. The demon was cursing at me in Jamaican patios. These are the translations: *"guwey"* means, *"go away"* and *"me gahne"* means, *"I am gone."*

(Incidents: Helped to Release Demons, 2/6/2010)

I emailed my manager and supervisor requesting unscheduled vacation for the week of February 8th, due to medical reasons. I later went to my friend, Donna's, house to spend the week. In the night, I woke up and I started saying, *"333,"* repeatedly; *"God, Jesus, Holy Ghost,"* repeatedly. My feet were crossed. After a while, I clenched my fist and put both hands in a V shape on my chest. I next moved forward as if to do crunches. All this time I was saying, *"RELEASED, never to return,"* repeated. Next, I moved my hands to both cheeks as I continued to repeat those words. I then held on to my belly with both hands and repeated those words. Next, I stretched and point both feet, repeating those words. I then focused on the left foot, rubbing away with the right foot and repeated the same words. While doing this, several demons responded, saying, "*never to return,*" repeatedly.

I called out rhinoceros, deception, goat, pig, ant, and others to see which one would respond. Spirit of deception spoke out, "*I deceived you. I will not return,*" repeatedly. After the foot area seemed clear, I started stretching my neck and head, saying, "*RELEASED, never to return,*" repeatedly.

The next day, in the morning, Donna told me that during the night, the Holy Spirit had her pulling away some of the evil spirits from me. I realized that this must have coincided with when I woke up in the night and was releasing evil spirits. Donna told me that her body was feeling terrible because she pulled the evil spirits onto herself. She said that she didn't know how I coped with so much. I told her that it must be due to the herb (God's herb) that my mother dreamt my sister about before my sister died (Reid).

I decided I would do another three-day fast. As usual, I read prayers from Charles Capps' book, *God's Creative Power Will Work For You.*" Afterwards, I released more evil spirits and demons by saying, "*RELEASED, never to return,*" repeated.

(Incidents: The Slippers Game, 2/7/2010)

Before going to bed, I said words which I realized evil spirits and demons did not like to hear; "*Do good works,*" repeatedly; "*Conform to the words of God,*" repeatedly; "*I have power over everything in my body,*" repeatedly." When I woke up later in the night to use the bathroom I saw one of my slippers faced down, even though I had left both faced up. Since I was feeling much lighter in my body I figure that some of them must have escaped and decided to use the slippers to scare me. I ignored it and went to the bathroom without it.

The next morning, I got up and found both of my slippers faced up, even though I did not put the other one upright, after I noticed it being faced down in the night. Again, I left the room to use the bathroom and came back to find both slippers facing opposite directions, even though before I left the room they were close together and facing the same direction. I realized that the evil spirits were trying hard to mess with my mind. I decided to borrow my friend, Donna's, slippers and leave mine for them to play with. They were failing in what they were trying to do.

(Incidents: Encountered Evil on My Journey, 2/9/2010)

The day before taking me to the doctor, Donna was attacked by evil spirit to try and prevent her from doing it. Instead, she got her husband to drive us to the doctor. On the way to the doctor, at one point I could smell the burning of goat. I put the water I had with me to my mouth for a while until it went away. Later on the journey, I got the smell of ants. Again, I used the water to my mouth and held it there for a while until the smell went away. I realized that evil spirits were also accompanying us to the doctor.

I told the doctor that evil spirits of the kind that talked was attacking me. He just smiled knowingly as if he expected me to say, *"unusual things."* I just thought to myself, *"Some professionals think they know all there is to know in their profession, but they are sadly lacking in many areas."* The world of *"spiritual interference"* in the lives of people is something, I believe, the medical profession is not exposed to, or know of but do not know how to handle.

However, this is something that affects their patients and, therefore, needs to be considered when treating them, as appropriate. I did not even try to convince the doctor of anything, since I was only interested in getting the medication so that it can help me with my sleep.

(Incidents: The Serpent Again, 2/10/2010)

I slept until about 11:00 a.m., while still at Donna's house. When I came to the kitchen I got a strong smell of ants. I realized that it was coming from one of the jackets, which was hung over a chair. I sat at the table on another chair. However, there was a strong sense of evil spirit from under the table, more like the serpent type I encountered before. I got up and decided to stay away from the jackets and the table as best as I could, throughout the day.

I called Donna at work and mentioned to her about the jacket. She was casual about it and said that evil cannot do anything in her house. She did not realize that they have different ways of entering a house. After all, I had carried a number of them with me inside her house. In the same way, they could attach themselves to her children's clothing to get entrance to her house.

In the early afternoon, Donna's husband and sons went outside to shovel snow since it was showing all day and a lot of snow had accumulated. One of her sons removed his jacket from the chair. Right away, I could tell the difference; in that, the strong smell of ants was removed.

After Donna came home late from work, she sat around the kitchen table. She called me to the table to show me something on her computer. As I bent over and spoke to her, I got the sensation of strong evil spirit going towards my head and mouth as I stayed and talk to her. Some of the sensations went to my legs. Again, I recognized this as the serpent type evil that I encountered before. I mentioned to Donna that there was the presence of evil spirit under the table. She responded that they cannot touch her. I knew that they would not touch her because she was not the intended victim. Those that send evil to others specifically assign the evil to the person they are after. You might be among other people, but if the evil was assigned to you, you would be the one to be attacked, and not them.

This incident made me realized that a Divine spiritual person (one who is gifted with detecting evil spirits and can communicate with God in the spirit) is not necessarily able to detect all forms of evils. I considered Donna to be at a higher spiritual level than me, since I had such an indication in a dream (Reid). Furthermore, she usually got more of a visionary revelation from God. I knew that I had spiritual shortcomings, in that, my spirit was not in alignment with my body and I have heard my spirit spoken out without me knowing that it was about to do so. I had assumed that whatever evil spirit I could detect, she would be able to do the same. However, I was mistaken. It is the Holy Spirit Who reveals things to you, individually or in group.

After the encounter with evil spirit from under the table, my head had a funny aching feeling; more at the center of my head, towards my forehead. I decided that later I would have to take out my weapon of God's word to address this problem. I knew I was dealing with a serpent evil spirit, based on my previous experience with serpent evil spirit behind a door. I started to say, *"Serpent evil, go now to a dry place and stay there until Jesus come, go now in the name of Jesus, you are unassigned from Jenness Reid."* After a while, it responded, repeating, *"Go now"* several times, and then left.

(Incidents: That Evil Bug, 2/16/2010)

The first day I returned to work after the weeks' vacation, I realized that evil spirit was awaiting me. I was at my desk typing on my computer between 9:00 a.m. and 9:30 a.m.

It Is Not Over

When I looked up to the left of me, I saw a brown bug. It was the size of a medium cockroach, but I did not recognize what type of bug it was. I quickly move away from the computer since I was very close to the bug. It was on the overhead cabinet next to the computer. It stood still as I closely watching it from a distance, not taking my eyes off it.

It was very unusual to see bugs at work. I remembered the experience that my niece, Rose, related to me two days ago in which she was told that the password was, *"In the name of Jesus Christ of Nazareth, touch not, taste not, handle not."* I started to say under my breath, *"In the name of Jesus Christ of Nazareth, touch not, taste not, handle not,"* repeatedly.

After a while, I decided to say, *"Go now in the name of Jesus to a dry place and stay until Jesus comes. You are unassigned from Jenness Reid, never to return. Go now in the name of Jesus."* As I completed saying, *"Go now in the name of Jesus,"* it started moving. I kept my eyes on it while I say, *"Go now in the name of Jesus to a dry place and stay until Jesus comes. You are unassigned from Jenness Reid, never to return,"* repeatedly, under my breath.

I was hoping that my supervisor whose cube was next to mine, would come so that I could ask him to kill the bug. After a while, the other supervisor, Godfrey, was passing by and saw that I was staring at something. He came to me and asked what was wrong. I showed him the bug. He asked me for tissues and I showed him where it was. He took some tissues and used them to kill the bug. He placed it in my garbage. I took the garbage and put it within the one in the ladies' room.

When I came back, Razan told me that he had seen a bug on the wall by the window last week when I was out from work. My cube was just a passageway away from the wall. I realized that the evil spirit in the form of a bug had come to my place of work, looking for me to do me harm. It had waited on my return.

The next day I heard that Godfrey was out sick from a stomach virus. He stayed out sick for the next two days. I realized that the evil spirit hurt Godfrey because he killed the bug.

(Incidents: The Presence of a Deceased Loved One, 2/19/2010)

Last night I prayed desperately for God to help me deal with whatever was surrounding Janet at work, which was giving me a suffocating feeling whenever I was close to her. She was my mentor, and this required that we work closely together, often. This day, as was the case most of the times, I felt the familiar suffocating feeling while I was close to her. I was determined to find a way to deal with it. While she was sitting at my desk, I repeated under my breath, *"Go now in the name of Jesus to a dry place,"* whenever I could do so without her noticing it.

After lunch, I went with Janet to her desk. I saw a picture of her with a man and a woman. I asked her if the woman was her daughter. She said, *"They are my daughter and son."* I said, *"So you have two children."* She said she had three but one died. I said, *"Oh, that's sad."* She then told me how it happened. He died at the age of seventeen and Janet took it badly. She was sick for a while.

I was overcome with grief for Janet. I started crying. She gave me a hug and said she was sorry she made me cry.

While Janet was relating the story to me I was saying under my breath, *"Go now in Jesus' name."* By the time she finished the story, I could feel a relief from the suffocating feeling surrounding her. I realized then that the suffocating feeling around Janet had to do with her deceased son being around her. From that day onward, the suffocating feeling I usually get whenever I was around Janet was gone.

I realized that I had successfully sent away the spirit that was attached to Janet. It was her deceased son. By his mother telling me his story and me reacting to it by crying, he was willing to leave his mother after I asked him to leave in the name of Jesus. God had answered my desperate prayer to *"help me deal with whatever was surrounding Janet at work and was causing me to feel suffocated around her."* It is best to rely on God to deal with any form of spirit. He knows them all and knows how to send them away. In my experience, what works for one spirit in sending it away does not necessarily work for the other.

(Incidents: Cloud of Darkness Disappears, 2/28/2010)

Before going to church, I was downstairs typing notes for my book when Kristal walked in. She said to me, *"I don't like the way you keep fixing your face. It doesn't look good."* I knew that I was not free from evil spirits, so I suspect that they did not like that I was writing about them and caused distortion of my face to show their displeasure.

I went to Dr. Bishop Hutchinson's church. He had two guest speakers for Black History month – a woman,

Catreen, and a man referred to as Apostle Gregory. Apostle Gregory spoke then Catreen followed. At the end of her preaching, she called on people to come up for prayers. I went, along with others. She called Apostle Gregory to come up and assist her. They went from one person to the other praying and laying hands on each. Apostle Gregory was the main one laying hands and praying.

When Apostle Gregory came to me he said that God had work for me to do for Him in this church. He said, "*A supernatural release is happening right now.*" He told me I should stand up and speak in the church. He said I should start thanking God. I started to say, "*Thank you God,*" repeatedly with my hands opened with palms up. My spirit took over and I started to say, "*Thank You,*" repeatedly.

After a while, I started stomping my right foot while saying, "*Thank You,*" repeatedly. Later, Dr. Bishop Hutchinson, told me that he saw a cloud of darkness just lifted from my head and went out the door, as my spirit was thanking God and stomping. The supernatural release had happened, as Apostle Gregory had said.

(Incidents: Spiritual Gas, 4/11/2010)

In the morning, I collected my mails from my house. In the evening, when I returned to Ruth's home, I opened the window in the bedroom slightly, since it felt a little stuffy inside.

I went downstairs, opened all the letters, and then sat down to do work on my netbook computer. After a while, I started to get a faint smell of ants mixed with a slight sweet smell, which was familiar. At the time, I did not recall what the sweet smell was. I was very focused on the faint smell of ants rather than the slight sweet smell because I was wondering if this was again an attack of evil spirit. I dismissed that thought. However, because I recalled Dr. Bishop Hutchinson's comment about me sitting at the same place all the time is not good, I decided to sit in a different chair.

I did not immediately get the sweet smell while sitting at the other chair. I continued working on my netbook computer. It didn't take too long before I started to get the faint smell of ants mixed with a slightly sweet fragrance. I decided that it was possible that this was the work of evil spirit, so I took my things and went upstairs, where I continued to work. I did not have any problems upstairs.

The next morning after the incident with the faint smell of ants and sweet fragrance, Ruth asked me why I left the bedroom window opened. I told her that I opened it because it was a little stuffy in the room the day before, but I forgot to close it. She then told me that she had a dream in the night, which was not too clear. Ruth dreamt that, *both of us were in a house. I told her to turn up the heat. She started to see smoke rising. She was not clear where it was coming from. She literally started smelling gas in the dream. She told me to turn off the stove. I came out of the room.* Ruth said she woke up out of the dream and then the smell of gas disappeared.

In the evening, I turned on the stove and since it hesitated before it was lit, I got the same slightly sweet smell that was mixed in with the faint smell of ants, yesterday. I then realized that yesterday's incident with me sitting in the chairs and getting the smell of ants and a familiar fragrance was a spiritual attack on me, using gas. God had allowed me to open the window in the bedroom so that the gas would not overpower me as the amount built up. The stove did not have any gas leak; but the enemy planned to use gas while we were sleeping to harm us. God alerted Ruth to the plot of the enemy, in her dream about gas.

Chapter 16

Research in Spiritual Psychosis

My experiences with spiritual attacks to inflict harm on me, anonymously, are much like someone hiring a hit-man to take your life or do damage to you with no connection to the perpetrator. This way, the perpetrator feels that the crime cannot be pinned on him, or her and, therefore, will be free from being prosecuted for a crime. After all, law enforcement is not equipped to deal with spiritual crimes.

In February of 2008, due to severe lack of sleep and extreme exhaustion from continuously fighting evil spirits, both in my dreams and in my awakening, I ended up in the emergency room and was diagnosed with psychosis, non-specific. I was hospitalized for about three weeks. Encountering and fighting evil spirits is not as uncommon as one might think. However, it becomes a problem when it is continuous because it affects the amount of sleep you get. Over-the-counter sleep medication will not help. At this point, you will likely need the help of a psychiatrist to prescribe medication that will mentally calm you so that you can rest. The problem is that the diagnosis might need to be re-categorized.

Before my hospitalization, I would get warning dreams from my deceased relatives (mother and sister). I must keep pointing out that before these family members died, God indicated to my family and me that they were going to die; when they eventually died, He indicated to us that they were with His saints; after this, He started to use them to give dreams to prepare us to fight against evil spirits that would be coming against us.

My family and I could not clearly interpret some of the dreams, but we figured that something was seriously wrong. Some of my relatives, especially Ruth, would also get dreams about me from our deceased relatives. These were also warnings about death, or something tragic, which we were not able to interpret properly. We could tell that evil was involved, because in a lot of my dreams I encountered evil spirit and fought, calling on Jesus.

All this finally lead me to a card reader who confirmed that I was being attacked by evil spirits; sent by someone who was seeking to break up my marriage. Later,

I discarded the help of the card reader after God sent me message, *not to mix His works with that of mankind. He was the One delivering me from evil spirit attacks.* Whatever, the card reader was giving me to ward off evil spirits did not help.

In my many experiences with encountering and fighting evil spirits, God, Jesus, The Holy Spirit, or God's angels are always there fighting for and with me, against the evil spirits. I would have dreams that served as warning from God before I had encounters with evil spirits. I also had awakening experiences where God allowed me to recognize when I was under attack by evil spirits. I have example of spiritual birds' attack, which connected a dream to awakening experiences.

On Monday night, July 6, 2009, I dreamt that, *my deceased mother told me that the problem between my husband and I were not over. She then showed me a wheel burrow with many black birds perched on top of it.*

After I saw the amount of birds, although they were many, I thought in the dream that with that amount, it would be over soon. I then found myself sticking the beak of one of the birds into a dead rat. I then put both on the ground and trampled on them, saying, "Step on the Enemy."

The next night, I woke up and could not go back to sleep. After a while, I literally saw the curtain being pushed out with a large object moving towards me. I recognized that it was evil and started defending my face with my hand, saying, *"Jesus conquers all,"* repeatedly. I continued to defend my face and say those words until I literally heard a flock of birds flying away. With the sound of birds flying away, I knew that the attack was over, and I stopped defending myself.

I had another connection to the above dream about flock of birds. Once, when my husband went away, I went back to my house and stayed with Sonia. The second to last day before I left, as I lay down to sleep, I saw a shadow passed by.

In the morning, I went out to get my car to drive to work. A large flock of small birds – about fifty, was at the end of the driveway. They were making extremely high-pitched chirping noises. As I got in the car and backed out, they flew up. When I reached the end of the road to make a turn onto the highway the same flock of birds was to the side of the road.

When I reached work, I saw three black birds perched on the building and a black feather was lying on the steps to enter the door. That evening when I returned to my house and parked the car, as I walked past the end of the driveway where the birds were perched, I heard the same extremely high-pitched chirping noise, even though they were nowhere in sight. This confirmed that they were evil spirits sent to harm me.

I recalled the dream I had with my mother showing me a wheelbarrow with small birds surrounding it and telling me that, the thing between my husband and me was not over. The next morning, the final day of staying at the house before my husband returned, again as I passed the end of the driveway I could hear the same extremely high-pitched chirping noise, even though birds were not present.

After the flock of birds' experience, God put it in my thoughts that psychiatrists need to distinguish problems caused by spiritual attacks. This kind of problem should not be categorized as *"Psychosis Non-specific."* I would suggest having the category, *"Spiritual Psychosis."* When God's children are under attack by evil spirits, He will defend them. There are many examples in this book. God wants His work to be more specific, hence *"Spiritual Psychosis"* would better indicate His works in the battle against evil spirits. There are other afflictions of people caused by evil spirits which do not end up in such fierce spiritual battles as I experienced. This is because the afflicted persons might not be aware of when they are under attack by evil spirits, hence their spirits would not fight back.

Spiritual encounters should not be categorized as psychotic episodes. Spiritual encounters could be purely from God, from Satan, or a clash of God with Satanic forces, which are attacking someone who God is defending. Spiritual encounters involving Satanic forces are the ones that bring about bodily sicknesses; physical, mental, and spiritual stresses. In moderate to severe cases, medical attention is likely required due to stress on the individual under attack.

The medical community must be aware that animals and objects are used by those who practice the art of spiritual wickedness (the practice of accomplishing devious works, using evil spirits). According to the card reader who I visited, animals and objects are used in spiritual attacks and not all who are attacked by evil spirit are able to detect it; you must be spiritually enabled to detect it. Some people end up in the mental hospital due to evil spirit attacks. Since they are not spiritually enabled, they were not able to detect what was bringing these attacks on and hence would not realize the root causes of their problems. On the other hand, if those who are spiritually enabled explain to others what is happening to them through the works of evil spirit, they too might be categorized as being crazy, if the person they are explaining the situation to are not spiritually enabled and hence can detect evil spirits. People will readily admit that their bodies have been invaded by bacteria or virus, but they are likely very hesitant or in denial that their bodies can be invaded by evil spirits.

I have learned from my experiences that God will stand against evil spirits and demons, in ways that may seem strange to some people, when they attack His children. As was in Biblical days, the works of God is incomprehensible to some people, even those who think of themselves as being *"well-learned."* It is interesting that God choses to reveal Himself to a card reader and a psychologist; to the card reader when she was using a spray to chase evil spirits away from me and my spirit arose and started repeating, *"In the name of Jesus;"* she joined me in repeating these words; and to a psychologist, when the Holy Spirit arose from deep within my chest as an enlightening force and settled on my face as I was relating to her that I had to call on the name of Jesus during spiritual attacks. That allowed the psychologist to inform me that my face lit up when talking about Jesus.

Just as the medical community learn to accept and work with other social issues, so too they need to learn about and work with the spiritually afflicted and the spiritually gifted. Advocates of other social issues have drawn attention to their situations, so too must the spiritually afflicted feel free to discuss their unusual afflictions. The Divine spiritually gifted should identify them as being spiritually connected to God (The Creator of Heaven, earth, and all things that exist). Those who claim to be spiritually gifted but are using evil spirits to carry out their works should give up this craft and ask God to forgive them.

I strongly believe that the medical community needs help in distinguishing medical afflictions brought about by evil forces from those that occur naturally. They also need help in distinguishing sicknesses brought about by spiritual disturbances from those of natural origins – physical or mental. With such help, the medical community would be better equipped to take care of their patients. They can establish the boundaries of what they can do to help individuals recover from negative spiritual interferences, such as those brought about by satanic forces.

Much like how the medical profession adapted to advances in technology, such as in the use of electronic medical records, so too must they prepare to deal with spiritual wickedness that have direct impact on their line of work. The hallmark of a scholar practitioner is to accept the reality of the experiences of others, strive to understand them, and work to see how they can find unique solutions to the social challenges that arise. After all, it is impossible for medical professionals to experience all that their patients are experiencing, so that they can truly relate to what they are describing. Medical professionals therefore need to pay attention to what I am pointing out here. We are entering an era in which God will be pouring out His Spirit on everyone (Joel 2:28-29). This means that individuals will become spiritually enabled; having dreams, visions, detecting when they are encountering spiritual attacks, etc. This includes medical professionals. All will be grateful that I am exposing spiritual wickedness, so that it can be dealt with publicly.

I had a car accident, which brought about back problems that I thought was solely due to the accident. The accident itself caused physical problems. However, I came to realize that the car accident was a cover for inflicting evil on me. The idea was that I would blame everything on back problem.

I can see where there is a need for training in the medical community to recognize when an apparent medical problem has spiritual origin. This would enable patients and families to better deal with the problems. They can seek the assistance of pastors, or religious leaders who Jesus Christ has given the authority to cast out evil spirits and demons, as was the works of Jesus and His disciples in Biblical days (Mark 3:7-15).

There is no need to go to card readers, or other such people who themselves might be the ones hired to inflict harm on you, by spiritual means. God has shown me that He will certainly equip His children with the power to overcome all forms of evil attacks. At times, this can be stressful, depending on the frequency and level of evil spirits, or demons with which you are dealing. You may also need medical assistance due to the stress, or exhaustion you are experiencing. The medical community needs to be able to identify when they should call on those who are truly operating under the power of *"The Holy Ghost [Spirit]."* Satan always come up with counterfeit activities to confuse the works of God. I know that God will be exposing the works of Satan so that His works will be distinguished. As how The Holy Spirit exposed Himself to a psychologist as I was telling her how I had to be calling on Jesus when I was under spiritual attacks, so will God be exposing spiritual afflictions being disguised as medical conditions.

As in my case, spiritual attacks can manifest themselves as other medical conditions and as a result, doctors might have a hard time explaining the condition, or finding a cure for it. This would likely result in the doctors feeling incompetent, or the patient feeling that the doctor is incompetent. Additionally, there would likely be excessive medical bills that the patient and insurance companies must pay, as was my experience.

The psychiatric community would do well to find a classification for individuals whose spirits have been awaken to detect when they are under spiritual attacks. Their experiences will likely seem strange to others, especially if they are not at the same level, spiritually.

Since we are God's creation (Genesis 1:27; 2:7) and God is a Spirit (John 4:24), we are composed of spirit, soul, and body (Genesis 2:7). Our spirits were made to commune with God. However, Satan and his angels are also spirits who were thrown out of Heaven and are living on earth (Revelation 12:9). Some devious people can use such evil spirits to inflict harm on others.

We are entering the era where there will be outright spiritual battles where God defends His children from attacks of Satan and Satan's angels. Both the church and the medical community must be prepared for this. It was for this reason that God allowed me to have exceptional dreams that caught my attention; prepared my family for something big to happen to me; and eventually informed me, through a dream, that I was ready to go on His mission, before I started to be aware of when I was under spiritual attacks.

Everything is perfectly timed by God. The time for the exposure of *"spiritual wickedness"* is here. God is using me to expose the *"spiritual wickedness"* that people think they can inflict on others and get away with – hands-off, no attachment to them, no charges brought against them, and no imprisonment.

Much like the movement to *"come out of the closet for gays and lesbians,"* so now is the time to expose the practices of spiritual wickedness, spiritual assault, and even spiritual murder. I know that I am not the only one that God has enabled spiritually to detect the presence of evil spirits. Each of us is given our own level of spiritual awareness and ways of detecting different levels of evil spirits. Let us embrace the fact that each of us has a spirit-self. It may be inactive, but present within the body. The natural person does not understand the ways of the spirit, unless God reveals it to him or her, or that person learns of it by some devious means. After all, the devil is competing with God to capture the hearts of people.

For those who are spiritually aware – meaning being able to detect the presence of evil spirits and being able to commune with God in the spirit, you are the selected minority who are empowered to expose the wickedness that some people do against others, through spiritual means. When the battle gets rough and you are physically and mentally exhausted, you might need medical help to get relaxation, as was my case, due to constant attacks causing severe lack of sleep.

Sometimes spiritual soldiers, doing battles, fight to the point of exhaustion. However, spiritual empowerment, given by God, is not something to remain hidden. Now is the time to identify yourselves as spiritual soldiers in the Army of the Lord and help to relieve those who are oppressed, suppressed, afflicted, and suffering due to evil spirits and demonic forces.

Some people obtain spiritual abilities by satanic means, with the intent of using it against others. However, selected children of the Almighty God receive Divine spirituality to counteract the works of Satan and to commune with God (Mark 3:14-15; John 4:24). Some people, even if they are religious, might be attacked by evil spirit without being aware of when it is happening. They suffer the consequence of such attack and try to find some natural way of explaining it.

Doctors should be aware that spiritually induced illnesses are likely to be out of the realm of their practice. It would be beneficial to their patients if they become aware of how evil spirits and demonic forces affect them. The patients would likely benefit from interventions by those capable of casting out evil spirits and demons, by the authority given to them by Jesus Christ (Mark 3:14-15).

Nee explained the concept of *"The Spiritual Man."* He indicated that a spiritual person is led by the Holy Spirit into spiritual reality, which allows his or her spirit to enlighten the mind. The human mind explains what becomes revealed to the spirit and put it into words for others to understand. The human mind might not be ready to accept matters of the spirit (1 Corinthians 3:1-2).

The mysteries of God are taught to human being by the Holy Spirit through the spirit, which He gave to us when we were created. As Nee further indicated, *"Not all Christians are spiritual"* (Watchman 96) since their minds are still in control, following things related to their bodies. They have two natures existing in them – the natural and the spiritual, each striving for authority over the other, daily. For the non-spiritual Christians, the natural is in authority. Under such conditions, their spirits are inactive. Baptism with the Holy Spirit releases the spirit of a Christian and enables him, or her to gain authority over the natural.

Intuition within the human spirit about things pertaining to God amounts to spiritual wisdom. Spiritual wisdom is attained through prayer (James 1:5). Once Christians' spirits are awakened by the Holy Spirit, they all have the same capabilities of knowing and using the words of God to do His works.

Possessing spirituality put us on equal level. Whether or not some of us are wiser, or more foolish, richer, or poorer in the natural realm, we are spiritually equal in the sight of God. We receive revelations from God through the Holy Spirit and spiritual understanding enables us to detect the movement of the Holy Spirit within our spirit. We know God's will through spiritual understanding (Watchman).

The medical community should at a minimum be required to take a course in spirituality that speaks to how patients can be affected by spiritual encounters. They should understand that we are spirit-beings and some of us are spiritually awakened to detect the movement of spirits – holy and unholy – within and around us. There are positive and negative spiritual encounters. The positive ones purely involve the works of God. However, negative spiritual encounters can be purely that of Satan, or a battle between Satanic forces and Godly forces; such as, God's angels, Jesus, and God's Holy Spirit Who comes to the rescue of an individual under spiritual attack. Spiritual enlightenment for all is key to identifying when a person is suffering from spiritual affliction and diminishing the practice of spiritual wickedness, as such practices become exposed.

Chapter 17

A Message to Church Leaders

My experiences with battling satanic forces serve as a warning to those who are children of God. It was clear to me that God had prepared my family to be of help to me during my times of war against spiritual darkness. God demonstrated that He is the deliverer of those who are caught in the grip of spiritual wickedness, not those who uses other means. He revealed this to others on two occasions; once when I went to a card reader for help to relieve myself of evil spirits, The Holy Spirit arose within me during the process, demanding evil spirits to leave in the name of Jesus; another time when I visited a psychologist for help, The Holy Spirit arose within me and lit up my face as confirmation to her that Jesus was the One helping me through my spiritual battles, as I spoke of this to her.

God will be very visible in His works against spiritual darkness. Now is the time to expose spiritual wickedness that causes afflictions, which are treated as natural sicknesses. Spiritual wickedness is carried out anonymously. God will expose such works through His anointed spiritual warriors and the confession of those who practice spiritual wickedness.

My experience with the *"666"* (rhinoceros) demon should not be taken lightly. Several months before this incident, God had my sister, Petra, give the bitter aloe plant to my other sister, Ruth, who put it at her kitchen window so that it could get light to grow. It all came together when I was under attack of the *"666"* demon and my spirit spoke out about tasting *"the bitter cup of salvation,"* referring to tea from the aloe plant. In many of the spiritual attacks, I had to declare myself as *"a child of God."* I concluded that we must be living in the era when Satan is set loose on earth.

The medical community is likely not prepared to deal with the effects of spiritual wickedness. I had been through medical condition that was thought to be of purely natural cause but could not be helped by the medical community. I found out that I am not the only one who had been through spiritual attacks. You only find this out from others if you first decide to tell them about your experiences. It was only after my eyes were opened to the involvement of spiritual afflictions and I started to get rid of evil spirits that my recovery from back problems progressed. The spiritual aspect of my back problem was being addressed; the natural aspect was different.

I sought help from a card reader during initial spiritual attacks because I did not know better. I soon cut off such a connection as I realize that whatever she gave to ward off evil spirits was not working; God was the One Who was really providing the crucial help in all the spiritual attacks. My encounters with the card reader gave me some idea of how these evil attacks came about. In later attacks, which were of a more serious nature, God connected me to a church bishop who was knowledgeable about fighting spiritual wickedness through fasting and prayer and waiting on God for instruction on how to deal with the different forms of evil spirits.

It would serve the church community well to enlighten the medical community about the effects of spiritual attacks on their patients. I know that through my experiences, God expect others to take heed of the evil days in which we are living. I promised God that I would help others who are going through similar experiences to what I went through.

While I understand that not all church leaders are called to be spiritual warriors for God, those who are so anointed should make themselves known so that they can better serve their communities. Now is the time to publicly acknowledge the existence of spiritual wickedness which has many ill-effects; for example, health issues, reduced productivity at home and at work, and more spending than for natural illness since doctors will often try several remedies for an ailment without really curing the patient. The gays and lesbian had their movement to bring to light their hidden existences. Likewise, as children of God who are targets of Satan's devices, we need to bring spiritual wickedness and battles to the forefront so that society can deal with such acts, openly.

Bibliography

Capps, Charles. *God's Creative Power: Will Work For You.* Harrison House, 1976.

Bevere, John. *Extraordinary: The life you were meant to live.* 1st ed. WaterBrook Press, 2009.

Nee, Watchman. *The Spiritual Man.* Christian Fellowship Publishers, Inc, 1968.

Reid, Jenness. *God Works Through Dreams.* Works Of Trinity, LLC, 2018.

The Holy Bible. King James Version. Holman Bible Publishers, 1979.